RE:THINKING

RE:THINKING

How to Succeed by
Learning How to Think

DANIEL COHEN

M. Evans and Company, Inc.
NEW YORK

Library of Congress Cataloging in Publication Data

Cohen, Daniel.
  Re, thinking.

  Bibliography: p.
  Includes index.
  1. Thought and thinking. 2. Success. I. Title.
BF455.C6729   153   82-1472

ISBN 0-87131-369-3   AACR2

M. Evans and Company, Inc.
216 East 49 Street
New York, New York 10017

Design by RONALD F. SHEY
Manufactured in the United States of America

9 8 7 6 5 4 3 2 1

for Peter Prochaska

Contents

CONTENTS

CONTENTS

CONTENTS

1

The Science of Thinking

KEYS TO THINKING—
UNDERSTANDING AND PRACTICE

Learning how to think is a two-step process. First you have to understand how your mind works, its strong points and its limitations. Then you need concrete and immediate advice and exercises that will help you improve your thinking skills. Without the basic understanding, the concrete steps are of limited value. You may find how to do something, but you won't know why, and therefore it will be hard for you to apply the techniques in a variety of situations. But the theory without the practical applications is equally limited. Thinking does not flow from the mere accumulation of facts; it's a skill that takes practice.

The aim of this book is to provide you with the most up-to-date and down-to-earth information about thinking, and with practical, simple, and often very enjoyable methods of improving your thinking skills.

RE: THINKING

Here are some examples of the kinds of situations this book will help you deal with:

• Your boss comes up to you and says your department is in trouble. Changes must be made. He asks for your suggestions, and your mind goes blank. What do you do?

• Your neighbor Roger is, in most respects, a pleasant, intelligent, and decent human being. But in the matter of politics Roger's views are stupid, meanspirited, and really quite dangerous. You have clearly pointed out his errors, yet he stubbornly refuses to recognize them, and he gets mad when you tell him. What's wrong with Roger? Or what's wrong with you?

• You are forty years old. You wake up one morning, look in the mirror, and say, "Where am I in life? What does it all mean anyway?" The questions are absolutely terrifying. Can you answer them? Should you try?

• You've just been offered a new job. The salary, working conditions, and all of the other objective elements of the job seem just fine. Yet you are uneasy. Something tells you not to take the job—that it isn't right for you. Should you listen to this "something" even though you don't have any good logical reasons?

• You have just heard a speech by candidate Joe Silverthroat. He's an impressive speaker, with charismatic appeal. But are his ideas sensible? Are his promises realistic, or is he just trying to mislead you with campaign rhetoric? Can you separate fact from bunk?

• Simon is always putting you down, making you look foolish. You're mad as hell, and want to retaliate, but you're afraid to argue with him, because he might make you look even more foolish. Should you keep quiet because you think he's smarter than you are? Or is there a way for you to speak up—and win?

• Janet says you don't understand her, that you never really

THE SCIENCE OF THINKING

listen when she has something to say. You think she is unsure, contradictory, and often evasive. Who's right, and what can you do about it?

• You are facing a difficult problem. You've turned it over in your mind a hundred times without coming to any satisfactory solution. Yet you still can't stop worrying about it. The worry is ruining your whole day. If you can't solve the problem at that moment, is there a way you can stop worrying about it?

• Your supervisor has just told you the project that you have been working on for weeks has been rejected. You have been asked to "think it through again." You're furious. "That SOB has never liked me," you think. "He'll never approve anything I do." Does that attitude make any sense?

• "Where there's smoke there's fire." "Birds of a feather flock together." "The exception that proves the rule." "Give 'em an inch and they'll take a mile." "Yeah, and you're one too." Should any of these phrases be part of your mental vocabulary?

• A fellow you know has tipped you off to what sounds like a great business deal. He has given you a stack of glossy brochures and reports to study, but he says you must act quickly. You don't understand the figures. What do you do?

• You've just had a fight with your children. They imply you are an old fogy who doesn't know what it is like to be young. You are sure that you know what is best, because you were once their age and you do know how it was. How can this dilemma be resolved?

All of these situations and many, many more demand that you think.

YOU MUST LEARN TO THINK

For quite a while now educators have simply assumed that all you had to do was go to school, and if you absorbed a lot of information, somehow you would automatically learn to think. That assumption has turned out to be quite wrong, and the problems spawned by that false assumption are now being felt.

In New York City, for example, there was great concern over a decline in reading test scores. The decline was considered a scandal and became a political issue, so a massive effort was made to improve reading scores. And the effort paid off, for test scores did improve. But while reading scores were going up, the ability to reason—to think—was going down. Learning to read and learning to think are not the same thing.

A recent Rockefeller Foundation report recommends that training in thinking be among the basic skills taught by all schools. The report recognizes the fact that thinking is a skill that can be learned. It is not something that grows inevitably out of the accumulation of facts. And anyone can learn to be a better thinker.

Thinking is not just an activity for the classroom or for the hours you put in at work. It is something that you must do all the time. The only question is whether you will do it well or poorly. If you can improve your thinking skills—and *anybody* can—it will help you improve in every part of your life.

Start learning How to Think right now.

2

Beating Your Biggest Thinking Problem

THE PROBLEM WITH PATTERNS

Your biggest thinking problem, and mine, and every-body's, is that our thinking becomes rigid. We respond to new situations and new problems with the same old ideas. Our thinking falls into a well-worn pattern—a rut. We tend to think in clichés.

The human mind is many things, but it is preeminently a pattern-making system. That's fine most of the time. In fact, it's absolutely essential. If our minds did not form patterns we would be completely immobilized by the huge mass of un-connected bits of information that press in upon us every hour of every day. This information has to be handled and organized in some fashion. To do this our minds create patterns.

But, like every other good system, the pattern-making properties of our minds can be applied inappropriately. They become, as the biologist would say, maladaptive. They don't work *for* us anymore; instead, they work *against* us. When this happens—and it happens all the time—we think of the same things and do the same things that didn't work before. We are on a mental road that always leads back to the same place. We experience a feeling of hopelessness. "It can't be done." "There is no solution."

There is an even more insidious effect of the pattern-making properties of the mind—insidious because we don't even know that something is wrong. We become satisfied doing something a particular way just because we have always done it that way. We never seriously think that there might be, and probably is, a better way of achieving the same goal.

When we think in patterns our mind automatically rejects anything that is not familiar and comfortable. How many times have you dropped an idea or plan because it was "unrealistic" or "silly," only to have that very same idea, turned into a success by someone else, come back to haunt you? I know it's happened to me. I'm sure it has happened to you too.

I once worked for a publishing executive who was famous for one thing: He had turned down a chance to buy *TV Guide* while the magazine was still small and struggling. He thought there was no future in a magazine of television listings. Why would anyone want to buy such a magazine when they could get the same listings in their local papers, he reasoned. So he passed the "unrealistic" idea by, and someone else bought *TV Guide* and made it into one of the greatest successes in publishing history. For the rest of his life this poor fellow was known for what he didn't have the vision or foresight to do. That's not what you would like to be known for.

From time to time you have probably been told to "get new ideas" or "think creatively," to take a "fresh look at the problem" or "be more open to new thoughts." However, you have also probably discovered that exhortations are not enough. You've already given yourself this same good advice. The trouble is, that's like telling a runner to "run faster" when he's just about to drop from exhaustion. The need to open up your thinking is clear—how to do it is not so obvious.

You do it the same way a runner would build up his speed and stamina, by exercise. Exercise and training improve the tone of the runner's muscles, the capacity of his lungs, and the efficiency of his circulation. It even improves his mental attitude. The more he runs, the more he knows he can run. That's true of any sport, and it's true of thinking as well. There are some simple exercises that you can do to help yourself break out of rigid patterns of thinking, to help you take a fresh look at things and get new ideas. You can train yourself to think more effectively.

THINKING OUTSIDE THE LINES

Before you can get to the solutions, you have to understand the problem. Most people don't really understand how rigidly patterned their thinking is, so I'm going to show you a variety of evidence that demonstrates this. There is a whole series of games and puzzles that depend on our rigidity of thought for their difficulty. Here is a familiar one. Look at these three rows of three dots each:

. . .

. . .

. . .

The instructions for this puzzle read, "Without lifting the pencil, draw four straight lines that pass through all of the dots."

You may have seen this particular puzzle before, for it is quite well known. If you haven't done it before, try it. If you have done it, try to remember how long it took you to solve the problem. Were you able to solve it by yourself, or did you have to look up the answer or ask someone? (If you can't figure it out at all, see solution at end of this chapter.)

When you finally do get the solution you may say something like "That's obvious. Now why didn't I see that at once?" How many times can you make the same sort of observation about everyday life?

The solution really is quite easy once you see it. Your mind makes the solution more difficult to see because of an unconscious assumption that all of the lines have to stay inside the "square" or connect a whole row of dots. But why? The instructions don't say that. We simply assume that the lines must stay within the square because it looks "right." We are used to seeing nice neat boxes. We attempt to impose that pattern on the puzzle, but it doesn't work. Unfortunately, that patterned way of looking at things keeps us from solving the problem; it becomes the problem.

FAMILIARITY BREEDS STAGNATION

Our inability to break out of thinking patterns has been demonstrated over and over again in laboratory studies.

In one study reported in the *Journal of Experimental Psychology*, psychologist Robert Adamson presented two groups of volunteer subjects with the same problem, that of

BEATING YOUR BIGGEST THINKING PROBLEM

mounting some candles vertically on a soft wooden screen. The subjects were given a number of familiar objects with which to accomplish this task: matches and a matchbox, thumbtacks, an eyedropper, tweezers, and so forth. The solution to the problem was to take a small box, in this case the matchbox, tack the candle to it, and then tack the box to the screen.

The subjects in one group were given the matches and matchbox separately; for the other group the matches were inside the box. Twice as many people in the first group solved the problem as in the second group. The people who got the matches inside the box tended to think of the box in its familiar role, as a container for matches. They had greater difficulty in seeing that it might be used for something else—in this case, a platform for a candle.

Repeated tests with a variety of different objects showed that most people have a great deal of difficulty solving problems that require using a familiar object in an unfamiliar way. For example, in one test the subjects were told that they could use any object in the room to solve the problem. The solution required the use of a piece of string. There was a piece of string holding up a picture in the room. Most people simply ignored it and were unable to solve the problem. They thought of the string as something that was holding up a picture. They could not think of it as being used for anything else.

In another study conducted by psychologist Adamson, subjects were asked to construct simple electrical circuits. They used either a microswitch or a relay in the construction. Later both microswitch and relay were available as items that could be used in making a pendulum. Those who had used the microswitch to build the circuit used the relay to make the pendulum, and vice versa. Using one of the items for one purpose made it difficult to see the same items being used as anything else. Even in these very simple tests the pattern-making properties of our minds are dramatically demonstrated.

THE FAILURE OF GENIUS

Fixed patterns of thinking do not affect us merely when we confront an individual problem. They may affect our entire life. This was brought home to me very vividly several years ago when I was talking to an old friend who is a physicist.

This fellow and I had grown up together. For as long as I can remember he had been considered a brilliant science student. When he entered graduate school (and our paths diverged) he had already become a scientific star, one of the most promising young physicists in the nation. All of those who knew him, including those who were in a good position to judge, thought that he was destined for greatness in his chosen field. Perhaps there would even be a Nobel Prize in his future.

When I met him again he was thirty-eight years old, and by all outward signs he appeared to be well on his way to fulfilling his early promise. He had a full professorship at one of the nation's leading universities. He published regularly in the scientific journals, and he was in demand as a lecturer and visiting professor at top universities and institutes all over the world. To me, the Nobel Prize seemed just a matter of time.

Yet when I talked to him, this apparently eminently successful scientist considered himself a failure and was deeply depressed about the prospects for his career and accomplishments. I tried to cheer him up by citing his many honors and achievements, but he merely waved them aside.

"Sure I'm a good teacher and a competent scientist," he said. "I'll always be that. But I haven't made any really important original discoveries. And now I'm too old to ever make any."

I was astounded, not only by what he said but by the absolute conviction with which he said it. "Old! Why, you're only thirty-eight. You're not an athlete or a male model, you're a scientist. You use your brain, not your face. You don't have to worry about wrinkles. Look at Einstein—he was the greatest scientist in the world when he was an old man."

My friend became irritable. "You're being misled by appearances. Sure Einstein was very famous when he was an old man. When you say 'great scientist' most people think of someone like Einstein, a man in his sixties or older, with a great shock of white hair. But that's misleading. Einstein did his really original work before he was thirty. The rest of his life was spent elaborating and refining his basic discoveries. By the time he was old his thinking in many areas had become quite rigid, and he was unable to accept many important new ideas—Heisenberg's work, for example—which later turned out to be correct.

"The young Einstein was an incredible genius, who revolutionized modern physics. The Einstein that most people think of, the old man with the unruly mass of white hair, was really behind the times."

He then pointed out to me that repeated studies had shown that most scientists did their important work before the age of thirty-four.

"So you see, I'm over the hill. I don't look it but I am. Oh, I'll be a distinguished faculty member and serve on all sorts of committees and advisory boards. I'll probably even pick up some prestigious awards along the way. But I'll never really do anthing first-rate or original. I know that now."

No wonder he was depressed.

RE: THINKING

Great discoveries in theoretical science do not depend as much on finding new information as they do on looking at old information or problems in a new way, or putting together what is known in a different way so as to achieve a new understanding.

The young mind, relatively uncluttered with deeply entrenched patterns, is more adept at doing this. The older mind, though it may possess more information and experience to draw upon, also has more deeply etched thought patterns, and thus tends to respond to problems along familiar and well-worn mental channels.

That is why children are better than adults at solving the popular Rubik's Cube puzzle. Says cube designer Erno Rubik, "It requires a certain innocence. The adult rejects many patterns because they have not worked out before."

This condition afflicts artists as well. Look at Pablo Picasso, unarguably the primary artistic genius of the twentieth century. Picasso worked in every conceivable artistic medium and style and mastered them all. Anyone who attended the Museum of Modern Art's overwhelming Picasso show will tell you that he exemplified virtually the entire history of modern art. Yet even this most original and innovative of artistic geniuses got old and rigid. Throughout the last twenty or thirty years of his life, though he remained physically and mentally vigorous and turned out a prodigious quantity of work, Picasso was for the most part repeating himself, or simply fooling around. His great days were over.

THE "IRRELEVANT" SOLUTION

OK, the problem is clear—what's the solution? How can we break out of our rigid, patterned ways of thinking?

Sometimes an unproductive line of thought can be broken

and a solution suggested by some apparently irrelevant occurrence, perhaps one that we are not even consciously aware of. That is the point behind the story of Sir Isaac Newton and the falling apple. Newton, one of the greatest scientific geniuses the world has ever known, was sitting under a tree thinking about the problems of the universe. Suddenly an apple fell from the tree and hit him on the head. This gave him the germ of the idea that led to his theory of gravitation.

It wasn't quite that simple—in fact, the falling-apple incident probably never happened—but the history of science is filled with accounts of authentic discoveries that were made because of seemingly trivial and irrelevant incidents.

This ability to use the "irrelevant" clue is not just the property of scientists; it is part of the mental makeup of all of us. A classic psychological test illustrates this point. The subjects were presented with a problem—how to connect two strings that were hanging from the ceiling. The strings were far enough apart so that if a subject got hold of one of them he was not able to reach the other. The solution was to attach a weight to one of the strings and set it swinging, so that it could be grabbed as it swings near the other string.

Some people were able to solve the problem without any help, but many were not. They kept trying to find different ways of stretching so that both strings could be grasped at once. They never thought of moving the strings. Then the experimenter walked into the room. He "accidentally" brushed against one of the strings and started it swinging a bit. That was the clue that enabled most of the previously stumped subjects to come up with the solution. Yet when they were questioned afterward, many of these people didn't know what it was that had tipped them off to the solution. As far as they were concerned, it just "came" to them.

HOW TO PLAY THE
RANDOM WORD GAME

The use of irrelevant material that breaks a mental pattern and leads to a solution to a problem is one of the principal techniques advocated by Dr. Edward de Bono. Dr. de Bono is a man of many talents. He holds degrees in medicine and psychology, he is an inventor, and his advice on thinking has been sought by governments and large corporations all over the world. Most of all de Bono is an educator, who trains people in what he calls "lateral thinking," which is also the title of his most popular book. The phrase is de Bono's, but as he freely admits, the concept is not particularly original, nor is there anything magical about using lateral thinking. We all use it from time to time, though not nearly as often or as successfully as we should. Some people naturally use lateral thinking very successfully without ever having heard the words.

Normal thinking, or vertical thinking, proceeds from one logical step to the next until a conclusion is reached. In ordinary speech when we say we have been thinking about something, that's what we mean. And most of the time that's just fine.

But sometimes vertical thinking is not the best way to approach a problem—sometimes it makes the problem worse, for as we have seen, the mind is a natural pattern-making system and when we concentrate on a problem our thoughts naturally tend to progress along certain well-worn mental paths. The lines have to be drawn inside the square; a matchbox holds matches and can't be used for anything else. Vertical thinking is analytical and excludes all irrelevant material. Therefore, in vertical thinking we tend to keep coming up with the same sort of answer. If it isn't a good one, we're stuck.

Lateral thinking differs fundamentally from vertical thinking. It allows for, indeed it encourages, all sorts of illogical jumps and movements. Lateral thinking is willing to embrace irrelevant material, to suspend judgment on the most absurd-sounding of ideas. In lateral thinking you play around with ideas and approaches for their own sake. "Let's suppose this matchbox isn't a matchbox, but something else."

Any method of stimulating new approaches can be used. Let's look at a typical exercise to train you in lateral thinking.

One way to get your mind working in new ways is to exercise it by random stimulation. Pick a problem, real or theoretical. Let's say the problem is how to cut down on window breakage and other school vandalism. Then pick a random word and see what thoughts the word will generate in terms of the problem.

You can use a table of random numbers (if you happen to have one) to select a page in a dictionary, or you can throw dice, or you can simply pick two numbers and find the word in the dictionary that way. Don't go through the dictionary looking for a word that will relate to the problem. That's exactly what you should not do. The word would not be random and you will slip into the old patterns.

I picked the numbers 835 and 11. On pages 835 of my old *Webster's Collegiate* the eleventh word is *parsley*—random indeed. Now let's see how that relates to school vandalism.

Parsley—vegetable—kids hate vegetables—kids hate school so they break windows—vegetables in school lunch—improve school lunches, improve attitude toward school—have meetings about lunches—get kids to participate—have meetings about vandalism.

Parsley—green—growing things—grow hedges around

RE: THINKING

school so that vandals can't get to it—use thorny plants—cut down hedges so that vandals can be seen—seeing vandals—improve lighting around school at night.

Parsley — green — garnish — decorations — put plants around school to make it look better so that kids will not feel like destroying it—get potential troublemakers involved in planting project—stimulate pride—have walls covered with ivy—would they throw rocks at an Ivy League school?

Parsley—parcel—piece—divide up the school into pieces or zones—make different groups responsible for watching their own zones—award prizes for the zone with the greatest reduction in vandalism.

Parsley — parcel — package — wrapping — protecting—wrapping the school building—new forms of protection—cover windows with plastic—gates over windows—guards at night—new alarm system.

Some of the ideas stimulated by the use of a random word may be obvious, others ridiculous or useless, and still others useful. They all might have been arrived at by straightforward vertical thinking. But that is not the point. The primary reason for such an exercise, and that's what it is, is to get you thinking in unusual ways. To break the mental pattern. To allow you to entertain strange ideas comfortably instead of rejecting them even before they can become consciously formed.

Most of us have, from time to time, engaged in the sort of free association demonstrated in this exercise. De Bono says that for this random word procedure to work effectively it cannot be forced—the mind must be given free play. Thus, he suggests that it be practiced for only three to five minutes every day. Pick a problem—anything from how to remove animal hairs from a rug to ways to improve the flow of traffic —then pick a random word. If you don't want to go to the dictionary every time, just pick a group of twenty or so random words, write them down, and put them in a bowl.

BEATING YOUR BIGGEST THINKING PROBLEM

When you are ready to think about a problem, pick one of the words.

When your three to five minutes are up, stop. Of course, you can't stop thinking, and for the rest of the day further ideas and associations may pop into your head. But don't spend the rest of the day trying to force more ideas from the word. That destroys the value of the exercise.

Use only one word a day. Otherwise you will be tempted to rush through a "difficult" word in the hopes that the next will be "easier."

As you practice this technique your ability to use it will grow. You will develop a quiet but firm confidence that something will come out of the exercise.

Random objects can also be used to stimulate ideas. The advantage to objects is that they can be looked at in many different ways and can thus stimulate ideas in many different directions.

Let's say that the random object is a newspaper. If you just picked the word *newspaper* you would probably think first of something to read, something that gives you the news of the day. But if you are looking at a real newspaper you might also think of the story that you see on the front page, a picture in the paper, the size of the paper, the kind of type that is used, what this particular paper happens to be resting on, the date of the paper, and so on. Random objects are capable of generating a large range of ideas.

The problem is picking the object. You have to try to make the selection truly random. If, for example, your problem was still school vandalism, and you picked a newspaper, your thinking might be dominated by a particular article you had read on the subject. A truly random object, say a glass of water or a comb, might prove far more useful.

Once again, three to five minutes of free thought. Then stop. Don't force it.

A few days or weeks of this practice is not going to turn you into a creative genius, and it's not going to solve all of your problems. But it can give you a good start down the road of breaking the patterns that so often shackle the mind.

WHEN HARD WORK
DOESN'T PAY OFF

Confronted with a difficult problem, the vertical thinker tries to collect more information in the hope that the accumulation of facts will give him the key to unlock the solution. All too often facts alone don't move him any closer to the solution. What is needed is a new way of looking at the facts. "You can't dig a new hole by digging a deeper hole in the same place," says de Bono.

Some people are naturally more adept at lateral thinking than others, just as some people are naturally better runners.

William is a young executive in a prestigious Chicago-based retailing firm. If you saw his well-tailored figure striding firmly down Michigan Avenue on his way to work in the morning, you would conclude that here is a young man destined for success. All the external signs point to it. He comes from a substantial and well-educated family. He was a first-rate student at a fine private university. His school grades as well as his IQ and other intelligence tests were far above average. When William was brought into the firm's executive trainee program he was earmarked for rapid promotion.

Yet, after a good start William's career has come to a standstill. His superiors know it and he knows it. The fast track that he once seemed to be on has suddenly become filled with obstacles and pitfalls. It has left the once confident young man angry, confused, and for the first time in his life profoundly unsure of his own mental abilities.

To make matters worse, William has to constantly compare himself to Brian, who entered the firm the same time he did. Brian is an indifferent dresser who walks with a decided stoop. He is not the image of the bright young businessman. He is the son of a Chicago cop and graduated in the middle of his class from a large and undistinguished state school. Both his grades in school and his scores on all the standard tests were average or only slightly above. How he got into the executive trainee program in the first place is a minor company mystery. Apparently someone had seen something in this unpromising figure and decided to give him a try. No one expected him to last six months.

At meetings William is always well prepared. He has thoroughly familiarized himself with all the relevant material. He presents his points crisply and listens carefully to what others have to say, taking copious notes. Brian, on the other hand, is not a particularly diligent worker. He is often poorly prepared, and spends a good deal of time playing with a pencil or staring idly at his shoes, but he has demonstrated a knack for coming up with the right idea at the right time.

One of Brian's almost casual suggestions saved the company $70,000 in a single year. Another resulted in an 18 percent reduction in employee thefts, and a third formed the basis for one of the firm's most successful promotional efforts.

William's suggestions are predictable and forgettable.

Brian has gotten the reputation of being an "idea man"—he is someone to be listened to, and someone so valuable that his idiosyncrasies can be overlooked. William has gotten the reputation of being a plodder—amiable and hardworking, but a plodder nonetheless.

The difference between William and Brian is not one of

basic intelligence. By every standard measure William is the more intelligent of the two. The difference lies in their ability to think. William's well-ordered thought moves in familiar grooves, while Brian's naturally disorderly mind breaks patterns, makes unusual connections and associations, and as a result comes up with new and often valuable ideas.

William's case is not a hopeless one, not by any means. He may never be the creative thinker Brian is. His chief talent may ultimately lie in working out practical applications for ideas thrown off by people like Brian. But William certainly would be able to make his thinking more flexible and creative. To make a comparison, I will never be the tennis player John MacEnroe is, but there is no doubt that with practice I can greatly improve my game and become a more than passable player. We know that about physical activity. We have yet to learn it about thinking. But you need the right kind of activity. You will not necessarily improve your tennis game by lifting weights.

THE "WHY" GAME

Here is a technique taken from a conversation that children often have with their parents.

"Why is the grass green, Daddy?"

"Because the green color makes the food for the plant."

"Why?"

It can drive you nuts, as I'm sure all parents know.

The child really doesn't know, and wants to find out. He wants facts. But in lateral thinking the technique should be used by adults not to find out information but to challenge basic assumptions.

For the game you need a partner. The partner doesn't simply repeat, "Why?" at the end of each explanation, as a

BEATING YOUR BIGGEST THINKING PROBLEM

child often does; he can question different aspects of the explanation.

"Why does a chair have legs?"

"To raise it up off the ground."

"Why does it have to be off the ground?"

"Sitting above the ground is more comfortable and more healthful."

"Why? The Japanese don't have chairs with legs."

How do you answer that one? Day in and day out you see chairs with legs, you sit in them. It seems the only natural way to sit. Now that basic assumption has been questioned. Perhaps there are better ways to sit.

Here is another one:

"Why should we vote?"

"Because voting is the basic right and responsibility of every citizen."

"Why?"

"Because it is the way we pick leaders to carry out the policies we favor."

"But why should I vote if I don't know what policies I favor?"

"Because by participating in the electoral process you learn more about the people and policies that govern the nation."

"Why? I never seem to learn anything during an election."

How do you answer that? Perhaps this person shouldn't vote. In any event, another basic assumption—that everybody should vote—has been questioned.

In life one certainly cannot challenge every assumption. Many things simply have to be taken for granted; otherwise we would be unable to live at all. But we cannot be strait-jacketed by assumptions. Assumptions are also tools in thinking. We must use them for our benefit. If an assumption or

RE: THINKING

a tool is no longer suitable, we must find a new one. You don't keep trying to use a broken pair of pliers or a hammer without a shaft just because you have had them a long time.

OUT OF THE MOUTHS OF BABES

Have you ever been surprised by a child's ability to get right to the heart of a problem? You find yourself thinking, "That child must be a genius." Not necessarily. The child may have a perfectly ordinary mind, but one that has not yet become rigid. Thus, children can often see the obvious when others cannot.

I have a magician friend who has spent a lifetime in the profession of fooling people. He contends that the more intelligent a person is, the easier he is to fool. The intelligent person is always looking for the complex and hidden, and is so convinced that he could never be fooled by the obvious that the obvious trick is the one he always falls for. As an example, he tells how he was once hired to work at an engineering convention attended by trained professionals, the tops in their field. These were the people who designed the highways, bridges, waterways, and other complicated structures upon which our modern civilization rests.

For the amusement of the engineers my friend created a pair of mechanical hands that did a variety of things, from picking up objects to waving at passersby. The mechanical hands were placed in the lobby of the convention hotel, protected by a glass enclosure. The hands were so proficient that many of the conventioneers stopped in amazement. They discussed among themselves the type of machinery needed to make the hands work. Some even took out pencil and paper to make preliminary calculations.

However, one of the engineers had brought his family to the convention. His son, a lad of about six, looked at the marvelous mechanical hands for about thirty seconds. Then he said firmly, "There's a man behind there."

And of course there was. The marvelous "mechanical hands" were really my friend standing behind a screen, with his hands, encased in metallic-looking gloves, stuck through the screen.

Obvious? Certainly. So are most illusions. But the engineers were so engrossed in their own particular way of seeing and thinking about the world that they failed to see what was perfectly clear to a six-year-old.

TURNING IT UPSIDE DOWN

Sometimes problems can be solved if they can be looked at from an entirely different angle or direction. Even looking at them backward can stimulate productive thinking. That's harder to do than you might think. Looking at things in reverse takes practice, so you should try to reverse as many situations as you can, as another mental exercise.

Every morning I take my large dog for a walk. My neighbor is sure to say to me, "Dog taking you for a walk again?" That's an obvious one.

Lights control traffic. Traffic controls the lights.

Mother takes care of baby. Baby fills mother's time.

Harry the fan cheering the team. The team playing for Harry the fan.

Going on a vacation. Having the vacation come to you.

All of these reversals contain at least a measure of truth or a different way of approaching a situation. But they don't have to be that sensible. They can even be quite silly. The point is not to make sense, but simply to do things differently.

Flying a plane. Flying without a plane. The plane flying you.

This particular technique works well in a group situation. An individual can usually think of only one or two reversals for each situation; a group can come up with many more, and, as always, one idea leads to another. Someone who does not have a single idea when first confronted with the situation may come up with two or three different ones after he hears what others have to say. This technique can be used as a teaching method or simply as a party game. Try it—it can be fun.

A couple of other techniques designed for the classroom will also work well in less formal groups, even at parties. Cut pictures out of a magazine or newspaper. Block out the captions. Then get people to try to figure out what is going on. (Don't use pictures where the obvious interpretation is dominant.)

Say you have a picture of a man in a business suit running down the street. Interpretations could be:

A man running for a bus.

A man running away from the police.

A man running from a burning building.

A jogger in disguise.

If the pictures are too obvious it is sometimes useful to use just half a picture and see what interpretations that will generate. The interpretation is less obvious, and people like to guess what is really happening.

You can take newspaper or magazine stories and try to switch them around. If you have a story that is favorable to a candidate, change all the references to make them unfavorable. If the candidate attracted a large crowd at a speech you can say the crowd was artificially inflated. If he was cheered at certain points, stress the statements that were not cheered.

Take a story and interpret it from several different points of view. Say the story concerns the escape of a bank robber from prison:

The prison guard may wonder how the prisoner got past him, and whether he is going to lose his job because of what happened.

The warden may feel that it is a good thing that the escape took place, because it is a dramatic example of the need for more prison guards.

The prisoner's point of view may be that escaping was a horrible error, because now he may be shot by the police.

The reporter who is covering the story may long for a shoot-out, because that would be a dramatic and newsworthy event.

It doesn't matter if any of these alternate points of view are true, or anywhere close to the truth. What matters is that they are different, that they show a new way of looking at a set situation.

That's what breaking mental patterns is all about.

EVERYTHING CAN BE BETTER

"Don't look for trouble." "Let sleeping dogs lie." These are maxims by which many of us are ruled. But to Edward de Bono they represent the wrong attitude as far as thinking is concerned. He says that people should stir things up and apply lateral thinking even when there is no apparent problem. One of de Bono's most important points is that we should periodically reassess everything that we take for granted—*everything*. We have to take a new look at things that seem "beyond a doubt" or "obvious." Things should be reassessed not because they are working badly, but simply because they have not been questioned for a long time. De Bono says that these reassessments are a "deliberate *and quite unjustified* attempt to look at things in a new way."

What is the value of such reassessments? Can't they be disruptive and perhaps unproductive? Not at all. They are a recognition of a simple fact: Nothing is perfect. Even when a system appears to be working well, there may be a better way of doing things. Yet unless and until serious trouble arises, we rarely question the system. "Let well enough alone." This is what de Bono means by "blocked by adequacy."

Ultimately, the most important use of lateral thinking is not in direct problem solving but in developing a flexible attitude.

TO SUM UP

We have covered some pretty important ideas here, so let's summarize.

1. The mind is a pattern-making system.

2. While patterned thinking is absolutely essential most of the time, it can also become your number one thinking problem.

3. Some people's minds are naturally more flexible than others', but everybody can improve their mental flexibility with practice.

4. Not all problems can be solved simply by accumulating more facts. Sometimes that just makes matters worse. What is often needed is a new view, or a new approach to the problem.

5. Nothing is perfect. Nothing is sacred. Every assumption can and should be questioned periodically.

BEATING YOUR BIGGEST THINKING PROBLEM

SOLUTION TO DOT PUZZLE

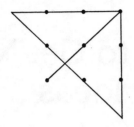

3

How to Get New Ideas

INNOVATION ON DEMAND

From time to time all of us are faced with the need to come up with a new idea, a new concept, or a different approach. This need can arise in our business life: "Sales are slipping, we must do something to stimulate them, the old approach isn't working anymore." Or it can come out of our personal lives: "I'm bored. My life is in a rut. I need to break out and do something different. But what?"

So you sit down and try to think of something new and different. Trying to generate an innovative idea can be a difficult, frustrating, and ultimately unsuccessful task. But it doesn't have to be. Most of us try to force the idea, rather than relaxing and opening our minds so that their full power can be used. We are also too negative, too judgmental, too quick to reject the unusual.

Let's compare two similar approaches to a problem, and

HOW TO GET NEW IDEAS

see why one works and one doesn't.

I have a friend who works in television. I'll call him Charlie, because I wouldn't want to embarrass him by using his real name. A couple of years ago he worked for a TV newsmagazine, a local news show patterned after the popular *60 Minutes*. Charlie had bounced around TV and films for years, and this job was the best he had ever had.

The show he worked on was highly respected. Charlie had a lot of responsibility, and a lot of freedom to do what he thought best. He should have been very happy and satisfied with his work, and he was—for a while. Then everything began to turn sour.

Ratings for the show began to drop, slowly but steadily. No one could figure out why. When the ratings first began going down, the general assumption was that everyone just had to work harder and do a better job at what they had been doing, and the ratings would recover. So everyone worked harder, but the ratings continued to sink. The staff began to get depressed and nervous. There were rumors of mass firings, or that the show would be cancelled altogether. Staff members were seen furtively reading the want ads at their desks.

The producers then decided that the staff had lost its "creative spark" and the show had gone stale, using the same old formula for stories over and over again. That, the producers assumed, was the reason the show was now losing its audience—it had become boring and predictable. So the call went out: "We need new, innovative ideas."

At first ideas were to be submitted in the form of memorandums—everybody on the staff was encouraged to write down new ideas. For a few weeks the "innovative" memorandums poured in. Most of them turned out to be the old ideas dressed up in new language, or an individual's long-held pet project that had been turned down before. The few genuinely new ideas were deemed unworkable or just plain stupid by the producers. But the pressure was always on to send in more memorandums.

From memorandums the increasingly desperate producers turned to meetings. Each Monday morning they would assemble the entire staff for a "creative meeting." Ideas were to flow freely in an informal setting.

"The first few meetings everybody plunged in with a lot of enthusiasm," Charlie recalls. "There was a great deal of positive energy flowing. Practically everyone contributed something. We were so anxious to speak our piece that we kept interrupting one another. It seemed as if the meetings had unleased a creative flood.

"But it didn't take long to realize that there really wasn't much happening. All we were doing was bringing up our old ideas again. And the producers sat around saying that this wouldn't work, or that this had been tried before and was lousy. They became very negative."

After the third or fourth session the meetings were punctuated with long periods of embarrassed silence, as the participants looked at one another, hoping that someone else would think of something to say. "It was absolute hell," Charlie recalls. "We would begin squirming in our seats. You could just see our bosses getting madder and madder. Finally one of them shouted, 'God damn it. You're all intelligent, creative people. Why can't you think of something? That's what you're paid for.'

"I felt pretty terrible. I tried, I really did. I think we all tried. But we were stuck in a mental rut. We were all like a bunch of little toy trains running on our own little circular tracks. Our ideas just went round and round over the same territory. We never got anywhere new.

"Those meetings were the worst part of the week for me—for everybody. I used to dread Monday mornings. You can't imagine how discouraging and draining they were. After the meeting I'd go out and have a good long liquid lunch. On Tuesday I would start worrying about what I was going to say next Monday. I wasn't even worrying about the show anymore; I half hoped it would be cancelled just so I could get out of those damn meetings. Absenteeism on Monday shot up."

As soon as another job opportunity presented itself Charlie grabbed it, though in many respects the new job wasn't as good as the one he was leaving. He got out just in time. The network demanded, and got, an almost complete staff housecleaning on the once popular show.

"I hate to admit it," Charlie says now, "but the new people got the job done. They really did come up with some fresh ideas. They were able to make the show more interesting and exciting without losing its original character, which had made it work in the first place.

"What really puzzles and bothers me is that I know most of the new people. There were no hidden geniuses. Our business is really a pretty small world. The new people were a good bunch, but they were no smarter or more creative than the staff I was on. There was probably less total talent. But they were able to do things we never thought of. Lord knows their ideas were obvious enough once you saw them. But we had agonized for months without any success. I guess it was their fresh perspective."

Have you ever had that kind of an experience? I certainly have. I once worked on a magazine where we never knew what to put on the cover. Every month we would sit down for a cover conference. Our boss would smile at us and say, "Well, what are we going to do this time?" We would spend the next hour or so trying to be brilliant. Sometimes I thought we came up with a good idea—sometimes not so good. After a while these cover conferences became harder and harder to attend. When I could, I would skip them by arranging to be out of the office.

Years later, when moving, I came across all of those old magazines. I laid them out on the floor, and I was amazed to see that all the covers looked pretty much the same. I remembered how we had labored and sweated over each cover, trying to produce something special and original. Looking at the covers years later, I realized we were never original. I also have to admit that the covers weren't very good, and that was reflected in the magazine's continually poor sales at the newsstand.

BRAINSTORMING THAT WORKS

Both Charlie and I had been taking part in a process called "brainstorming." In its simplest form brainstorming takes place when a group of people sit around and toss out all sorts of ideas and suggestions concerning a particular subject or problem. The aim is to generate new solutions through a free flow of ideas. It's not a new technique at all. About twenty or so years ago brainstorming became something of a fad in many major corporations. One company had a special "brainstorming room," in which everything was yellow— the walls, the rugs, the tables and chairs, even the note pads (and, of course, the pencils, though the lead presumably was black). Yellow was thought to stimulate the mind.

Edward de Bono, the apostle of lateral thinking, believes brainstorming is an extremely useful way to generate new ideas. Yet the brainstorming sessions that Charlie and I had engaged in were frustrating, depressing, and profoundly unproductive. Why? Because just sitting around in a room tossing around ideas isn't good enough. You need rules and formal conditions.

HOW TO GET NEW IDEAS

That may seem like a contradiction, for lateral thinking involves the production of informal ideas. But most of us are really quite uncomfortable with this kind of thinking. Ours is a world in which most people believe that there is only one "proper" way to think, and that is to proceed in a step-by-step way. Anything else is "not serious" or "childish." We feel inhibited in blurting out what might seem like a wild and even ridiculous idea. "What will other people think?" "Will I sound foolish?" This is where the formality of the setting comes in.

Let me make an analogy. Most of us would feel foolish if asked to go to work one day wearing an outrageous costume. We would even be inhibited about dressing up at Halloween, when people are supposed to wear costumes. But if we are invited to a fancy-dress party where everybody comes in costume and there is real prestige attached to wearing the most bizarre or unusual outfit, our inhibitions break down. It's the same with outrageous ideas. In a setting where they are expected and appreciated, they come more easily. But the proper formal setting does not require yellow walls or rugs.

Here are the rules for a productive brainstorming session: The ideal size of the group for such a session is about a dozen. Larger groups (fifteen or more) become unwieldly, and some individuals are overlooked and never get a chance to contribute. Smaller groups (under about six people) tend to break down into arguments between individuals or factions.

The session needs a chairman to enforce certain rules. The chairman is supposed to guide the session, not direct or control it. The lack of an effective chairman is perhaps the primary reason why the brainstorming sessions in which Charlie and I were involved broke down so badly. Neither of our groups had a formal chairman, but our bosses were present—in his case the show's producers, in mine the magazine's editor. There was a natural tendency to tell the boss what he wanted to hear. Certainly no one wanted to present something that obviously conflicted with one of the boss's cherished ideas, or an idea that the boss was known to hate. Thus, the main aim was not getting new ideas, but pleasing the person with the power.

The chairman's most important job is to keep the members of the group from criticizing or even evaluating the ideas presented by others. That's not easy to do. My editor was trying his level best to be "open-minded." But it's hard to keep from expressing an opinion, either by word or by look. The completely nonjudgmental chairman would have to practice his job.

It is up to the chairman to define the problem. If the problem is too broad (a solution to the energy shortage) the discussion is likely to be too diffuse to be of much value as training in lateral thinking. If the problem is too narrow (a more equitable vacation schedule for the shipping department) it is likewise not going to produce the most useful sort of training exercise. Somewhere in between these extremes the chairman must find a suitably stimulating topic. The choice might be something like "Design a better doorbell."

The chairman has to control the session, not allowing one person with a particularly loud voice or aggressive personality to dominate the others. People are not pushed to contribute unless there is a prolonged period of silence. The chairman can also suggest his own approaches to the problem, though they are not to be taken as orders or directives.

While the freest flow of ideas is encouraged, there have to be some boundaries to the discussions, and the chairman must keep pulling the participants back to the central problem. This, de Bono acknowledges, is an extremely difficult

HOW TO GET NEW IDEAS

and sensitive task, since apparently irrelevant flights of fancy can often lead to useful suggestions. (Indeed, this is one of the basic premises of lateral thinking.) Still, if the subject under discussion is a new kind of doorbell, and people begin coming up with suggestions on how to solve the Middle East crisis, the chairman must exercise his authority and bring the participants back to the problem at hand.

One of the participants in the session must agree to serve as a notetaker. While the person who occupies this position must have a legible handwriting, the notetaker is not a court reporter who has to take down everything that is said—a verbatim transcript is exactly what you don't want from a notetaker. A brainstorming session might be tape-recorded for later playback, but that does not eliminate the need for a notetaker. It's the notetaker's job to jot down all the significant and new ideas that are generated—no easy task, since it means that often nebulous and poorly stated ideas must be reduced to an understandable summary.

A good part of the notetaker's value is to help the speaker clarify his ideas. At any point the notetaker may hold up the session until he can catch up, or ask if a particular summary in his notes is correct. If he has misunderstood or misrepresented what the speaker said, then it is up to the speaker to restate his idea and perhaps offer his own summary. When in doubt as to what to put down, the notetaker should ask the chairman.

When the discussion seems to come to a halt, or is getting too far off the track, the chairman can call on the notetaker to read back the ideas that have already been given.

There is to be a distinct time limit on his brainstorming sessions. They should never run more than forty-five minutes, with about thirty being optimum. In some cases twenty is quite enough. It's the chairman's job to bring the session to a close. The temptation to carry on too long when the session seems to be going well must be resisted. I can testify from personal experience that the untimed brainstorming session can become sheer torture. The participants are fatigued in mind and body (thinking can be hard work!) and yet they are still being called upon to produce. In my experience, the less productive a session was, the longer it was likely to go on, in the vain hope that if everybody sat around long enough and thought hard enough some marvelous (or at least adequate) idea would appear, as if by magic. The result of this is prolonged discomfort.

For people who are not used to this type of formal brainstorming, and even for some who are, a brief warm-up session is suggested. For about ten minutes before the main session begins, the participants can deal with some simple problem—the old saw about building a better mousetrap would do. The warm-up not only shows people how the session is run but reassures them that no matter how far out or ridiculous an idea may sound, no one will exclude it and the participant will not be laughed at. On the subject of mousetraps someone might suggest that the need for traps could be eliminated entirely if the mice were made into pets. The suggestion sounds silly, but is perfectly valid in a brainstorming session.

When the full session is finished, particularly if it has not been overlong and exhausting, it is quite natural for the participants to continue thinking about the problem, and to continue to have ideas about it. The chairman should tell all the participants to submit a list of additional ideas if they wish. The notetaker's notes can also be copied and submitted to each participant, with instructions to add any additional ideas he may come up with. Each brainstorming session should have a follow-up.

It is during this follow-up that an evaluation of the ideas takes place. No evaluation can or should take place during the session itself, because that discourages new ideas and would basically change the nature of the session. Yet some ideas clearly are good and others absurd, or outdated, and still others, while not useful in themselves, might suggest fruitful approaches to the problem under discussion or to other problems. Often ideas that look as if they should have been thrown away at once have developed into something of significance.

BUILDING A BETTER DOORBELL

For a better understanding of how brainstorming can work, here is part of a simulated brainstorming session. The comments of the chairman are presented in parentheses () and those of the notetaker in brackets []. The subject being discussed is how to design a better doorbell.

Don't use a sound, when someone presses the button on the front porch a light flashes on in the house.

Have it set up so that all the lights in the house flash on or off. No matter where you are you will know that someone is at the front door.

Have a dog that is trained to bark whenever someone steps on the front porch.

Keep a flock of geese in your front yard. They will honk every time a person enters the yard.

[What do I put down here? Geese as an early warning system?]

How about an animal warning system? Any sort of animal that makes noise would do.

You could have an electric eye in the front yard that rings a bell whenever someone passes a certain point.

A television camera trained on the front porch so that you can see a person before you open the door.

(I think that we're getting a bit off the track here. That's more of a security system than a doorbell.)

RE: THINKING

How about two bells? One out in the open that would be for salesmen and bill collectors. The other would be hidden and only your friends would know about it. A person might not want to answer the public bell.

A bell with a switch you can turn off to avoid interruptions.

A bell that plays a tune that you can change.

(You mean a bell that activates a tape recorder or record player?)

That's an idea, but I was thinking more of chimes or a music box that would play "Jingle Bells" at Christmas and "Happy Birthday" on a person's birthday.

Something that gives the visitor a recorded message, saying that a person is not at home or doesn't want to be bothered, or tells the visitor where the person is.

[Would that be a phone-type recording device?]

Why not? The visitor could leave a message as well as receive one.

Do it visually. A recorded message could be flashed on a TV screen near the front door.

The button could activate a robot that would come to the front door and greet a visitor.

[Would that be a robot door answerer or robot butler?]

And so on and so on. The variations, while not endless, are far greater than most people imagine before they sit down and try this form of brainstorming. Remember, the aim is not necessarily to come up with a suggestion that is useful or practical at this point, but to come up with suggestions that are novel and different and that might result in new ways of looking at the problem.

If done properly, this kind of brainstorming not only provides excellent practice in lateral thinking, it can be a lot of fun as well.

DON'T THROW IT AWAY

As you can see from comparing the good and bad examples of brainstorming, one of the principal differences is the attitude of the leader of the group. Charlie's boss and mine were negative, quick to reject unusual ideas, and even to put down those who suggested such ideas. The result was inevitable. The creative flow was shut off. People were afraid to say anything really different. The clear idea being communicated was that different is wrong. In some ways that is a microcosm of life: We grow up being told that to think differently is wrong. The natural pattern-making qualities of our mind are encouraged by our upbringing.

The leaders in brainstorming groups should be entirely nonjudgmental. One of their primary functions is to keep ideas from being dismissed out of hand. Even if an idea seems entirely unworkable at the moment, it may come in handy later, or it may lead to useful ideas in other areas.

The importance of not dismissing something out of hand cannot be overemphasized. History is filled with ridiculous ideas and chance occurrences that resulted in great discoveries.

Take the discovery of penicillin. In 1928 Alexander Fleming was an obscure teacher and medical researcher in London. He had been working on various types of antiseptics. As part of his work he grew bacteria cultures in small glass plates called petri dishes. One of his cultures became contaminated —a mold spore drifting in the air had settled on the bacteria culture and was growing there. It was a common enough accident, and the culture was certainly ruined.

What would you have done? What would I have done? We probably would have looked at the dish, muttered, "Oh

RE: THINKING

damn," then thrown away its contents and sterilized the dish. But Alexander Fleming didn't do that, and it's a good thing for all of us that he didn't. The mold growing on the bacteria seemed to have some interesting properties, so he decided to experiment with it. The result was penicillin. How many lives have been saved by Fleming's decision to consider the unlikely—to explore an odd bypath? It is impossible to speculate how long the discovery would have been delayed, but for Fleming's decision not to throw it away.

This discovery was so unlikely that it was years before other scientists recognized it. Fleming kept trying to tell people what he had, but they wouldn't listen. After all, molds had never been used to cure anything before.

Edward de Bono considers the ability to hold off final judgment on even the most unpromising of ideas one of the cornerstones of his whole philosophy of thinking. He has even invented a new word that he gets his students to use in their thought and daily life. The word is *po*—it's somewhere between *yes* and *no*. It can't be defined exactly. The closest one can get is to say it is a special form of *suppose*.

Po is needed, says de Bono, because our pattern-making mind tends to quickly accept or reject an idea. It's yes or no—and once that decision is made, alternative ideas and trains of thought are cut off. Even impossible ideas can be held with use of the word, just to see where they will lead.

Let's say a group of businessmen are discussing the sale of grommets. Grommet sales have been dropping steadily. No one seems to know what to do.

One of the brash young men in the group says, "Since we can't sell them, why don't we give them away?" His older, wiser, and more powerful colleagues look at him as if he were a madman or a heretic.

"You don't stay in business by giving things away, Johnson."

Abashed, Johnson slumps down into his chair and does not say another word during the conference. Of course, his idea is never even considered.

But let us say this group of businessmen were all familiar with the theories of Edward de Bono. Then it might go quite differently.

Johnson would say, "Po, why don't we give them away?"

Instead of rejecting the idea and freezing Johnson out, the others would stop and consider, see where the idea led.

"Perhaps if we distributed them free more people would realize how useful our grommets really are, and that would lead to sales in the future."

"Getting rid of the grommets would free a lot of warehouse space. That would save money."

"Giving away the grommets would generate a lot of publicity for the company."

Perhaps the idea really is useless and leads nowhere. But with *po* it isn't rejected out of hand. Everybody accepts the use of the word and the concepts it implies—a whole new way of thinking and of making decisions, a more flexible and creative way. You don't need to use "po"; it isn't a magic word. What you *do* need is the idea behind it. Don't throw it away; hold off judgment and see where it will lead.

HOW TO USE A BRICK

There is a simple psychological test that you can turn into an exercise in breaking mental stereotypes and getting new ideas, or into a party game. It's called the Unusual Uses Test. The test consists of taking an ordinary object and seeing how many different uses for it an individual can come up with in five minutes.

Let's say that the object you chose is a brick. There

are the obvious uses: for building and throwing. Then there are less obvious uses: Break it up and write on sidewalks with the pieces; heat bricks and use them to cook food. One youngster who took the Unusual Uses Test said a brick could be used as a bug hider: "Put the brick on the ground for a week. Pick it up and see what bugs are hiding under it."

Try the exercise with some of the objects you find in your room. But the same warning must be issued with this test as with all the others—don't force it. Go your five minutes, then stop. Don't immediately look around the room for another object so that you can better your score. There is no score. It's just another way of training your mind to look at things in a different way and get new ideas.

If you are not used to thinking this way, you probably won't come up with a lot of unusual uses at first. The patterns are deeply furrowed into your mind—a brick is a brick is a brick. You may find yourself thinking, "This is silly," or "It couldn't possibly be used for that" or "Who would ever need something like that?" Just relax. The more times you perform this exercise the more adept at it you will become. And it will help free your mind.

An interesting variation on the Unusual Uses Test is the Impossible Situation Test developed at the University of Minnesota. You can't do this by yourself, but it's fun to try in a group. Take an impossible situation and see what the consequences might be.

What would happen if we could become invisible at will?

What could happen if a hole could be bored right through the earth?

What would happen if we understood the language of the birds and animals?

How many consequences of such a situation can you list in five minutes? Try it with these examples. It's a real mind-stretcher. Since you start out with the impossible, your solutions just can't be obvious. As before, there are no "correct" answers—just different ones.

Does all this seem a bit silly and impractical to you? Well, remind yourself that not so many years ago it seemed silly and impractical for grown men and women to dress up in shorts and sneakers and run around for hours. Yet today no one doubts the physical and psychological benefits of jogging. And the lone runner is no longer jeered at.

SUMMING UP

Once again we have covered some pretty basic ideas, so let's repeat the high points:

1. New ideas can't be forced; they must flow freely.

2. The greatest killer of a new idea is a negative attitude. "It won't work." "It can't be done."

3. Even if an idea seems utterly impossible it should not be rejected out of hand. It may stimulate other ideas that can lead to a solution.

4. With practice you can improve your ability to come up with new and creative ideas.

4

How to Understand Other People

OTHER PEOPLE—OTHER WORLDS

How often have you felt like this:

"She doesn't understand me. She's not stupid, and I've told her time and again. But she just doesn't see it. Does she have some sort of mental blind spot, or is she deliberately twisting my words?"

That's a common enough feeling—and a dangerous one. It has led to everything from divorce to war.

The first principle that you are going to learn from this chapter is that she (or he) probably really doesn't understand you and does not see things the way you do. Yet she is not stupid, blind, or guilty of deliberate distortion.

Each of us exists in our own mental world. While my world is in many respects similar to yours, they are not identical. What you see as pretty I may see as unattractive. What is an obvious fact to you may be news to me.

HOW TO UNDERSTAND OTHER PEOPLE

There is no way of getting around this fundamental fact of human existence. The differences are biological necessities. But there are ways of handling these differences effectively. They don't have to result in mutual incomprehension and anger. There are ways of expanding our own mental world so that we can understand others better.

The reason that we all live in our own mental world is that our minds and memories are highly selective. All of us are assailed daily by an enormous variety of stimuli—sights, sounds, feelings, and ideas—everything from random noise to radio and television reports, from deeply felt personal experiences to vague insubstantial rumors.

It's too much. The mind can't handle it all. To make some sense out of this great avalanche of stimuli the mind has to be selective. Scientists have found that the mind usually selects what it wants. That is why what you see is not necessarily what I see, and vice versa.

THE COCKTAIL PARTY EFFECT

The most dramatic and frequently cited example of selective perception is what has been called the "cocktail party effect." Imagine a large cocktail party. The room is filled with guests grouped in little conversational knots. In addition, there is the clink of glasses, the rattle of plates, and some traffic noise filtering in from the street outside. The total of all of this is a constant murmur in which no individual word or sound can be distinguished at a distance. Yet if someone across the room mentions your name, even in a voice that does not appear to rise above the general murmur of background noise, you are very likely to pick it out. That's the cocktail party effect. The mind simply selects from the babble just those sounds it is most interested in.

RE: THINKING

The cocktail party effect always intrigued scientists, so it has been tested in dozens of different ways over the years. Mothers can pick out the sound of their own child's voice from the voices of scores of screaming children in a playground. People can sleep through many loud noises but certain sounds that they are attuned to—a child crying, the motor of a particular car—will wake them immediately, even though the sounds that they slept through were much louder.

And the cocktail party effect isn't limited to the ears. We also see what interests us. Writing in the *Journal of Abnormal Social Psychology*, social scientist Morton Wiener described how he tested his subjects with fuzzy carbon copies that contained words that had both a sexual and a nonsexual use (such as *fairy, screw*). Before the carbons were given out some of the subjects were exposed to those words in a sexual context, while others saw them in a neutral context. Those who had been exposed to the words as sexual more rapidly identified them in the fuzzy carbon copies. They saw what interested them.

SEE NO EVIL, HEAR NO EVIL

If we often hear what we want to hear and see what we want to see, it is just as common not to see what we don't want to see and not to hear what we don't want to hear. This proposition, too, has often been tested. Volunteers are given stimuli just below the conscious perceptual level. For example, a person may see a variety of images flashed on a screen. The images appear so quickly that they are barely registered consciously. Yet most people have an easier time seeing and reporting images that they find pleasant or neutral than they do perceiving disagreeable or threatening images.

HOW TO UNDERSTAND OTHER PEOPLE

The different reactions show up in the pupils of the eyes as well. When someone is looking at pleasant materials the pupils expand measurably. Conversely, looking at distasteful or disagreeable materials produces contraction. The contraction or expansion of the pupils is entirely involuntary.

The same experimental results hold true of sound. We tend to hear what we find pleasant more easily than what we find unpleasant.

We also all have a strong tendency to see and hear what we need or want *even if it isn't there*. The classic experiment in this area took place way back in 1948. Psychologists took a group of volunteers and divided them in half. One group was given lunch; the others were kept waiting until they were hungry. Then both groups were shown some vague pictures—actually just smudges. As by now you might expect, the hungry subjects saw food objects in the picture, while the well-fed subjects did not.

When people look at an object they interpret it according to their interests and experience. In a study by Alvin Scodel and Harvey Austrin reported in the *Journal of Abnormal Social Psychology* a group of Jews and non-Jews were shown 100 photographs of faces and asked to pick out the photographs that looked the "most Jewish." The Jewish subjects rated a larger percentage of the photographs as Jewish than did non-Jews. However, among the non-Jews were a number of admitted anti-Semites, and they too rated a larger percentage of the photographs as Jewish. The subject was on their minds.

Even something as simple as perception of size can be dramatically influenced by mental predisposition. In a classic 1947 study, groups of children were shown coins and then asked to estimate how large the coins were, compared to different-sized disks. All the children tended to overestimate the size of the coins somewhat, but children from poor families thought that the coins were far larger than did children from well-to-do families.

A REMEMBRANCE OF THINGS PAST

The great French writer Marcel Proust wrote a series of seven novels that is titled in English *Remembrance of Things Past*. That's fine for literature, but in reality recapturing the past is a hopeless task, for if we see and hear what we want, we are even more apt to remember what we want.

British psychologist F. C. Bartlett wrote a book called *Remembering*, and after citing many experiments and studies he concluded that we hardly ever remember things as they were. What we remember is things the way we think they should have been. Bartlett found that what he called "effort after meaning" caused us to work on our memories until they conveniently fit the patterns that already existed in our minds. This is not a conscious or deliberate act of falsification; it seems to be almost an automatic one. "Remembering," Bartlett concluded, "is an imaginative reconstruction or construction. . . . It is hardly ever exact."

Even short-term memory is highly inaccurate and selective, as every policeman or trial lawyer knows who has tried to get a straight story out of an eyewitness.

A little demonstration that is sometimes conducted in law schools makes the point perfectly. The professor is standing and lecturing as usual. A stranger enters the room, interrupting the class. He speaks to the professor, and a sudden violent argument erupts. The stranger pulls out a pistol and shoots the professor, who falls to the floor. The stranger rushes from the room. The whole sequence of events takes place in sixty seconds or less, far too quickly for any of the students to do anything but sit in stunned silence, eyewitnesses to a violent crime.

Of course, it's all an act. The professor hasn't been shot, and the "murderer" is an upperclassman picked for his acting ability.

As soon as this is explained to the students, a questionnaire is passed out among them. They are asked a series of simple, factual questions about the incident—such things as, what was the stranger wearing? Did he have the gun in his hand when he came in, or was it concealed? Who was the first to get angry? Did the professor push the stranger?

Though this inquiry is conducted within minutes of the event and all the witnesses are intelligent individuals who should be good observers, they invariably get a high percentage of the questions wrong. We don't remember what we see, and what we do remember is highly selective.

Preconceived notions influence what the students remember seeing. If the "murderer" is a black man, black and white students tend to recall the incident quite differently. If the professor was unpopular, there is a greater tendency to report that he, not the "murderer," started the argument, or that he pushed the intruder.

This demonstration of the gross inaccuracy of our memories can also make for an interesting parlor game. You can stage a "murder" for your guests. Gather them all in one room. Of course, don't tell them what is going to happen; that would put them on their guard, and you would no longer get their natural first reactions. Pretend that you have called them together for quite a different reason. Then have someone rush in and "shoot" you. Pass out the questionnaires and see what your guests remember. The results will be enlightening to both you and them.

Another test of how our preconceived notions influence

our memories uses a drawing showing a variety of ethnic types riding in what looks like a subway car. Subjects are given a short time to look at the picture and then the picture is then put away and the subjects are asked to describe it as accurately as possible. Though the picture is neutral, many people describe it in terms of ethnic stereotypes. For example, the black man is often said by whites to be holding a knife or razor—when in fact he has nothing in his hands.

THE PITFALLS OF MEMORY

So far we have been talking about short-term memory, trying to recall what we saw or heard just a few moments earlier. That's quite bad enough. Long-term memory is worse —far worse. A lot of the incidents that we remember about our early life simply never happened the way we remember them. Sometimes they didn't happen at all. What we recall is not what actually happened, but what we think *should have* happened. It is genuinely unsettling to realize that the pictures of our past that each of us carries in our head are, in Professor Bartlett's phrase, "an imaginative reconstruction or construction." Unsettling, but nonetheless true.

Living in an "imaginative reconstruction or construction" is not altogether unpleasant. Reminiscing about "the good old days," even (or especially) if they were nowhere near as good as we remember them being, is one of life's pleasures as one gets older. However, we must be extremely careful not to confuse these reminiscences with reality.

A great deal of the conflict that arises between generations results from the older generation's inability to accurately remember what it was like to be young. "In my day we didn't do things like that." Well, perhaps, but don't bet on it.

WRITE IT DOWN

From time to time I have lectured throughout the country on various subjects that border on the psychic or paranormal. Almost invariably after one of these talks someone will come up to me and say that he is sure he is psychic. Then he will rattle off half a dozen or so events—a death in the family, a major disaster, the recovery from a serious illness—that he had premonitions about. He had a hunch that something was going to happen, and then it did.

For such individuals I have a simple piece of advice: Write it down. Next time you get a hunch or a premonition that something is going to happen, write it down. Then put the paper away. In six months or a year, read over what you wrote. This little exercise often disabuses people of the notion that they are psychic.

The written record usually reveals many premonitions or hunches that didn't come true. When we rely on memory we recall only those that did. It also generally shows that even when there is a "hit," or correct prediction, the case is not nearly as clear-cut as one recalls it. Subtly and without our consciously being aware of it, the mind alters the prediction to fit what actually happened. But there can be no mental alteration of the written word.

The advice "write it down" need not only apply to those who think they are psychic. Anyone who is truly interested in his past should use it. Keep a diary—I know that's an old-fashioned suggestion, but it works. If you want to be more modern, record the day's events on tape. In either case you will be getting down what happened close to when it happened. If you rely on your memory your memory will obligingly tell you what you want to hear. It will alter the events to suit your preconceptions.

The degree to which this can be done is absolutely astonishing. My mother and I still argue good-naturedly about whether I had a pet alligator. She insists I did, and I am quite sure I did not. I know I wanted one, and constantly pestered her for one, but as I remember it, she never gave in. I did have a variety of strange pets, including several kinds of reptiles, but I feel certain I would not have forgotten a creature as singular as an alligator. Who knows?

How many times have you been absolutely certain that a particular thing happened, only to have someone tell you, no, it didn't happen that way at all, it was very different? The difference in recollection can be more than a matter of interpretation; it can be in matters of hard and indisputable fact. Either I had an alligator or I didn't.

THE NOT-SO-POWERFUL MEDIA

While we unconsciously select what we see, hear, and remember, we also exercise a great deal of conscious selectivity.

Do you read the *New York Times*? The op-ed page, the page opposite the regular editorial page, has columns and articles on different subjects written by people with widely differing points of view. At the bottom of each article is a little biography of the writer. Do you find yourself reading the biographical note first, before you read the article, to see if you are likely to agree with the writer? If you are likely to disagree, do you skip the piece altogether?

If you do, you are typical. Studies of newspaper reading show that we tend to read only those articles and columns

HOW TO UNDERSTAND OTHER PEOPLE

that we already agree with or are interested in. We skip the rest. In watching television or listening to the radio we pay close attention only to those stories we find congenial. The stories that tend to contradict our beliefs we will watch fitfully and remember poorly. If a story we don't like really intrudes itself on our consciousness, we just shut the TV or radio off. Neutral stories are interpreted according to our desires. Or, as a survey of the effects of the media by sociologists John and Matilda Riley put it: "A person, whenever he is free to do so, choses to read certain messages or listens to certain programs and not others. In general, whether he is aware of it or not, he listens to what he wants to hear and reads messages in support of what he wants to believe."

Far from turning to the news as a source of information from which to make up our minds, we turn to those portions that support our beliefs. People who are neutral or don't have strong feelings on a topic don't pay much attention at all to it. People who don't vote also don't read newspapers or listen to news programs.

Social scientists Raymond and Alice Bauer put the matter even more strongly in an article in the *Journal of Social Issues*: ". . . the reasonable conclusion to reach in any given instance . . . is that any correlation between communications behavior and the personal characteristics of the people involved is a result of *selective exposure*, rather than evidence for the effects of communications." People who read conservatively oriented publications chose them because such publications fit their political orientation. Reading the publications did not make them conservatives.

This may not hold true in societies where the sources of information are limited, but even in totalitarian societies the effects of propaganda may be grossly overestimated. George Orwell's nightmare novel *1984* postulated a society in which people's thoughts were almost entirely controlled by an efficient and all-embracing propaganda apparatus. It is almost 1984 now, and while totalitarian societies still exist and the people in them are often ignorant of much that goes on in the outside world, the type of total thought control that Orwell envisioned has not come to pass.

In a society such as ours, where information constantly comes at us from all sides, we are simply unable to absorb it all. We pick and choose, selecting what we want to see and hear. As a result, even in our open society people can find themselves in a position where they are essentially exposed to only one point of view. At least, there is only one point of view they absorb—the one that they are already predisposed toward.

A person rarely faults the media when they report something he agrees with. He begins to denounce the "power of the media" only when they report things he doesn't like. Then he can ignore the unpleasant information and think only about the "power of the media." He can even blame "the media" for the existence of the unpleasantness they are reporting.

All of this casts considerable doubt on one of the most popular bugaboos of the day—the power of the media. We are repeatedly told that we the public are a bunch of dumb sheep who can be swayed this way or that by a clever columnist or a silver-throated anchorman, but the overwhelming scientific evidence points in the other direction. Far from being swayed, we pay attention only to those opinions we already agree with.

Of course, the media can exert an influence on people's opinions—but the influence is far less than most of us imagine, it is slow to take effect, and it is far from being universal. This is particularly true in regard to deeply held basic opinions—those beliefs and ideas that really count.

PREACHING TO THE CONVERTED

Dwight Moody, a popular nineteenth-century evangelist, was often a frustrated man. He would look out over the well-dressed, clean, and thoroughly respectable throng that regularly attended his meetings and complain, "I see too many Christians out there."

Moody's passion was conversion. He wanted to bring the unchurched back to church, to reform the drunkard and the libertine. That was the point of all his talks. He wanted to change people's minds. But his audience didn't need the message he brought. They were regular churchgoers. They had heard it all before, and they already agreed. They had not come to the meeting to be converted, or changed in any way. They had come to have their beliefs reinforced.

If one of the drunken wretches toward whom Dwight Moody pitched his message had actually shown up, he might well have been run off by other members of the audience who feared the scoundrel would disrupt the orderly proceedings. At the very least the poor fellow would have felt out of place in the crowd. Yet the whole elaborate enterprise had supposedly been organized for people just like him.

Follow-up studies of the conversions or "decisions" made at various evangelical meetings confirm the observation that on such basic matters as religion change comes slowly. Most of those who walk up to the front of the hall when the call is made were regular churchgoers before they entered the hall. Some are carried away by the enthusiasm of the moment. Others feel that their religious practices have slipped a bit, and want to have their beliefs reinforced by the public act of making a "decision." Still others are young people who feel the walk down the aisle is an important ritual one must go through.

RE: THINKING

Among those who were poor church attenders before the meeting, some will begin to attend more regularly, but in a short time the vast majority slip back into their old habits. The long-term conversion of the hardcore sinner is a rarity.

This problem of "preaching to the converted" has troubled not only preachers but politicians, the supporters of a variety of causes, and anyone who has tried to change the minds of large numbers of people. You may be able to physically deliver your message to people, but it is hard to get them to listen or read, and even harder to get them to change.

Among the most successful political groups today are the so-called single-issue groups, which use highly selective mailing lists to reach a targeted audience. They bombard people with appeals, magazines, bulletins, brochures, and whatnot. Though much of this material does contain information, the primary aim is not informational. These groups are not trying to tell the people on their lists anything new. They are not trying to convince them of anything. The aim is to energize those who are already supporters—to write letters, to give money, to vote a certain way. Trying to change a lot of minds would be a waste of time and money.

Where then do our basic and well-defended ideas come from? There can be no simple answer to that question. Some come from our families and the people we grew up with. They come from our neighbors and friends, from the experiences we have had, from our education, and to a degree from the information we encounter from day to day on television and in the newspaper. In short, they come from lots of places. You can't just blame television.

THE PSYCHOLOGICAL BASIS
OF DEMOCRACY

It's nice not to be a sheep, an individual whose opinions are so weak that he can be swayed one way or the other by the fashions of the moment, or by the last person talked to. On the other hand, since the information that filters into our minds is extremely selective, we can become very narrow. But there are some techniques for breaking out of this narrowness. They will help you understand other people.

1. Professor Antony Flew, the author of *Thinking Straight*, suggests that you collect statements from people you normally disagree with. "And these must be statements which, when made, were contemptuously disbelieved by you and by other opponents, but which nevertheless turned out to have contained the truth and nothing but the truth."

2. Once a week—and more often if you have the time—read the whole newspaper: all the editorials, news articles, and columns. Those you normally agree with and those you normally disagree with. Make a special effort to read those you disagree with.

3. Subscribe to at least one journal of opinion that you are likely to disagree with strongly. For example, if you are a liberal the *National Review*, a conservative *The Nation*. Read it, trying to be as open-minded as possible.

4. Cultivate friends and associates of different outlooks, religions, and political ideas. But don't—repeat, *don't*—try to convert them or have them convert you. Don't even discuss your differences. The purpose of this activity is to show that people can think very differently from you and still be good and decent human beings. Concentrate on your similarities, not your differences.

RE: THINKING

5. Finally, and this is the most important of all, *be tolerant.* Remember that the people who disagree with you are not necessarily evil, or stupid or bad in any other way. They may genuinely see and experience the world differently from you. Tolerating a wide variety of difference not only makes good psychological sense, it is the main principle upon which our nation was built. Unfortunately, we tend to forget that sometimes, and it's good to be reminded.

5

How to Profit from Being Wrong

IF YOU CAN'T BE WRONG
YOU CAN'T BE RIGHT

You could be wrong.

That's a simple statement but a profound one. Our whole system of rational thought is based on that very simple premise.

It's easy enough to say "Of course, I could be wrong," far harder to accept it than most of us think, particularly in regard to basic or strongly held ideas. You may say "I could be wrong" but you don't really mean it.

Here is the basic test of rational thought that you can give yourself—and others. It is technically known as the "criterion of falsifiability." You ask, "What evidence would be needed to prove this belief wrong?"

The criterion does not apply in matters of faith or other beliefs that lie beyond the scope of reason, but it does apply to any beliefs we hold that we consider reasonable, rational, logical, or scientific. In fact, you can use it to separate the different kinds of beliefs. We often contend that a certain idea we hold is rational when in fact it's not. Apply the criterion of falsifiability to your basic beliefs and see how they hold up. You will probably be surprised to realize that much of what you believe is a matter of faith.

Says Professor Nicholas Capaldi, the author of *The Art of Deception*, "It is almost a definition of rationality to say that a man is rational to the extent that he will tell you under what circumstances he will change his mind. To know when a belief will be considered false is to know how to reason with someone who holds that belief."

It is also to know how to reason with yourself.

HOW YOUR MIND
DEFENDS ITSELF

Admitting that you could be wrong is difficult because it runs contrary to the way the mind usually works. We have stressed the fact that the mind is a pattern-making system. Once a pattern—an idea or belief—becomes fixed in our neurological pathways, it is extremely hard to alter it. The more basic the belief, the more we refer to it in our thoughts, the more well worn is that particular neural pathway—and thus the harder it is to change the idea, even when it is wrong.

This is not necessarily bad. You don't want to have such flimsily held opinions that you sway with the wind. But to have all your ideas so entrenched and hedged around with defenses that change is impossible is hardly a desirable situation either.

GOOD RULES—FOR OTHERS

We have little trouble recognizing irrational or immature thinking, faulty reasoning, and downright fanaticism in others. We do not see the same sort of thinking in ourselves. From the inside all of our own deeply and passionately held ideas and convictions seem obvious and beyond dispute. It's all those others who are making the mental errors.

In doing research for this book I came across an excellent little volume on rational thought. Carefully and skillfully the author explained how arguments and propositions can be examined and weighed. In most ways it is an eminently rational and intelligent work. Yet, in virtually every example the author chose to illustrate a point he displayed an overpowering political bias. He could have chosen some of his examples from the other side of the political spectrum. The author himself pointed out that even your opponents can sometimes be correct; apparently *his* can't. He could have gone outside of politics entirely to choose his examples—but no. This book is not meant to be a political one, and the strident tone is particularly out of place in a work that is supposed to encourage the weighing of different points of view.

I suspect that the author was quite unaware of what he had done, and if questioned would insist that he had displayed no bias at all, but was simply using the best factual examples at hand and simply being honest and truthful. Which only goes to show that in the area of rational thinking there can be a great gap between theory and practice, and that our mental defenses are really quite ingenious and powerful. And usually we are quite unaware of them.

Defense is all well and good, in its place. But we are all too often keeping out not the enemy, but new and potentially

RE: THINKING

valuable information and the chance to form new ideas. Our defenses allow us to continue in the belief that we are always right, a destructive and dangerous delusion.

So we are going to look at five of the most common of these mental defenses, to find out how to spot them in ourselves, and how, when necessary, to combat them.

1. SHIFTING THE GROUND

There is one type of mental defense that is exceptionally dangerous and potentially destructive. Not only does it keep you from examining the argument at hand, it can lead to some very ugly consequences. It's called the "subject/motive shift." Let's see how it works in a situation that you have probably encountered in your personal life.

Sam and Brenda were having an argument. It started as a discussion but it soon became an argument. At first Brenda laid out all of her positions calmly and rationally.

Sam strongly disagreed, but instead of offering counter-arguments he said, "Let's get down to what the real problem is here. You're really angry at me and that's why you're saying these things."

That is a textbook case of the subject/motive shift. Sam shifted the ground of the discussion from the question at hand to Brenda's motives. As you might imagine, at this point Brenda blew up, and that's when the really nasty argument started. Naturally Sam now was convinced that his observation was correct, because Brenda really was mad at him. In effect, Sam won the argument without ever having touched the question. In reality, both Sam and Brenda were losers, because this maneuver opened up a personal gap between them, and still the original subject of the discussion had never been touched.

The subject/motive shift is a very effective defensive maneuver, for it avoids all discussion of facts that may not necessarily support your point of view, and it puts the other person on the defensive. In this case Brenda's counterargument was to question Sam's motives, and so it went round and round, both of them getting angrier and more personal, and further and further away from what was supposed to be the subject.

The technique is insidious, because once you use it you never have to question your own views. The focus rests entirely on the other person's motives. You start with the assumption that you are right and if anyone disagrees there must be something wrong with them. There is no doubt that in many discussions the real fuel of the controversy is some unstated personal reason. But so what? If there are facts to be dealt with, the other person's motives may not be of much importance. And remember, questioning another's motives will inevitably be regarded as an attack. The other person will immediately go on the defensive. That is when things can get out of hand.

So rule number one in dealing with the subject/motive shift is, don't do it. Whenever possible, stick to the question. That can be uncomfortable. It can even mean losing an argument. But that's a very small price to pay.

The same mental technique is often used in public as well as private matters. You turn on the television set and there is some guy saying a lot of things that you strongly disagree with. "Who is that guy anyway?" you think. Then you find out that he is a spokesman for an organization that you dislike and distrust. "Aha," you conclude, "that fellow's nothing more than a mouthpiece. He's paid to say all those things." Once you have successfully settled on the man's impure motives you feel secure in not having to listen to another word he says.

Rule number two is, listen anyway. It's certainly helpful to discover a person's motives for saying something, but

RE: THINKING

motive isn't everything. You could be wrong and your opponent right. It's necessary to examine the statements themselves. Even people we dislike may sometimes say things that are true or useful.

Be honest with yourself. In most cases the subject/motive shift is just an excuse for not listening to what someone else has to say, not questioning what you already believe.

2. YOU'LL NEVER BELIEVE ME

In the classic subject/motive shift you don't have to listen to what someone says because you question his motives. The reverse is what might be called the "you'll never believe me" technique. In such cases you assume that the other person isn't going to listen to what you have to say, so you're not going to bother to say it.

"I'm not going to explain, because you never listen."

"Don't try to tell him anything, people like that are immune to reason."

While it is quite true that a lot of people don't listen to what others say, and explanation can be an exercise in futility, it isn't always true. You have to be careful that this kind of avoidance isn't an excuse for hanging on to a weak argument without having to expose it to challenge. If they'll never believe you anyway, you don't even have to bother to talk about the subject, or think about it.

You must ask yourself a hard question: "Why won't they believe me?" Is it because they are hopelessly biased, or is it perhaps because what you have to say isn't worthy of belief?

A variation of this particular maneuver is the political statement "I'm not going to stoop to respond to a charge like that."

3. CHANGING THE RULES

Let's say you hold a very strong belief that a certain thing never happens. Then it does happen. What do you do? Admit you were wrong and say, "Well, I guess it does happen sometimes"? Or do you try to change the rules in order to show that you were right after all? You probably try to change the rules.

The town in which I live holds an annual volunteer firemen's parade. It has been going on for a long time and is the biggest single townwide event of the year. Almost anyone will tell you, "It never rains the day of the fire parade." Since the parade is held early in July, a normally dry time of year, the vast majority of the parades have been held on hot and sunny days. But *never* rains? Not quite. When it does rain the rain is called a shower or a drizzle—not rain, though at other times of year the same amount of precipitation would certainly be called rain. It would be accurate to say that it rarely rains, or that it has never rained hard enough to force cancellation of the parade. But that lacks the thrust of *never* rains. So we simply change the rules, and what would be rain any other day of the year is something else on the day of the parade.

There is the case of the return of the buzzards to Hinckley. Every spring all of the buzzards are supposed to return to this midwestern town on a particular day. It's a local festival. The buzzards do return at about the same time every year, but over a period of several days. How does the myth survive? Simple—the rules are changed. All of the buzzards that appear before the appointed day are called "scouts"; all of those that show up later are "stragglers." Only those buzzards that show up on the appointed day are called "returnees."

Antony Flew calls one variety of this rule-changing

maneuver the "no true Scotsman move." He tells the apoc-
ryphal tale of a proud and patriotic Scotsman who sits down
to read his favorite sensationalist tabloid and finds the story
"Sidcup [England] Sex Maniac Strikes Again." After absorb-
ing the shocking but gratifying details, the reader concludes
firmly, "No Scot would do such a thing!" A week later the
same paper carries the even more scandalous account of the
doing of a Mr. Angus MacSporran in Aberdeen.

Now our proud and patriotic Scot is presented with a
dramatic counterexample. He should reexamine his original
position, or at the very least decide that *most* Scots would
not do such things.

"But even an imaginary Scot is, like the rest of us human;
and we none of us do what we ought to do. So what in fact
he says is 'No true Scotsman would do such a thing.' " Once
again the rules have been changed in mid-argument. And the
imaginary Scot does not have to admit that he is wrong.

That is the no true Scotsman move. You will perhaps
recognize examples of it in your own thinking. Flew's example is an obviously humorous one, but this sort of thinking
can be very unhumorous and frightening.

Just a few weeks ago I was watching a televised interview
with a Ku Klux Klan leader in Connecticut. The interviewer
happened to be a black reporter, and as you can imagine, the
situation was tense. The Klan leader was saying how there
were two types of blacks. The "colored folk"—they were the
ones who worked, went to church, and knew their place.
Then there were the "niggers"—they were the ones who
didn't want to work, and stood around on street corners
drinking cheap wine and causing trouble.

The reporter, who was beginning to have difficulty
controlling his temper, pointed out that as he had come into
town he had seen quite a number of whites standing around
on the street drinking and being loud and abusive.

"Oh," said the Klansman confidently, "they're just white niggers." That is the no true Scotsman move in its purest form.

This last example should provide you with evidence of just how dangerous this sort of evasion can be. It will allow the most dogmatic and fanatical of people to support their ideas in the face of clear evidence to the contrary, simply by changing the rules to fit their ideas.

In thinking, don't change the rules just to save an idea. It's far better to admit that you are wrong—or at least to reexamine, and possibly alter, your original position.

4. EXCEPTIONS AND RULES

One of the most common methods of avoiding or evading an uncomfortable fact is to fall back on the familiar saying "It's the exception that proves the rule."

Let's say that you are having a discussion, common among cat owners, as to which are more affectionate, male or female cats. "Male cats," you assert positively, because you happen to have a very affectionate male cat.

It is then pointed out to you that the cat that is currently sitting in your lap purring contentedly is a female, whereas the animal huddled in the corner snarling and spitting is a male. "Ah well," you say, "that's the exception that proves the rule."

The example is a frivolous one. The point is not, for it is simply astounding how many times that phrase comes up, and how often it is meant to serve as a convincing argument. Yet if you think about it for a moment the phrase is absolutely stupid. If the exception proved, or verified, the rule, then it follows that the more exceptions there are the better the rule, and that the rule that had nothing but exceptions would be the best of all.

In fact, this hoary phrase, which was first used by the

philosopher Sir Francis Bacon (1561–1626), has been completely misunderstood for centuries. Back when Bacon wrote, "to prove" meant to test. What he was saying was the exception *tests* the rule, or that you can test a generalization by looking for exceptions. The exceptions don't validate or prove the rule in the modern sense at all—quite the opposite.

This complete and rather foolish reversal of Bacon's meaning has become firmly entrenched in our language and thought because it is very useful in protecting preconceived notions. We need it to protect ourselves when a firmly held belief is threatened.

The phrase "the exception that proves the rule" is one that simply should be dropped from your vocabulary right now.

5. YOU CAN'T PROVE A NEGATIVE

All sorts of wild rumors and theories float around.

President Kennedy was assassinated by the Mafia.

The U.S. government has conclusive proof that UFOs are spaceships from other planets, but is covering up this information.

The final Fatima prophecy revealed that the world is going to be destroyed by the year 2000, but the Church refuses to make the prophecy public.

You have probably heard these rumors and many others. Perhaps you have even been tempted to believe them. So many others seem to. A plausible-sounding case can be constructed to back these rumors, and many others—that's why they become widespread. Often these rumors appeal to some of our basic beliefs or feelings: a distrust of the government, a gloomy or fearful view of the future, or the sheer excitement involved in believing that things are not what they seem.

When you ask for the evidence to support these various rumors and theories, it usually consists of pointing out holes in other theories, and a few odd bits and pieces strung together with a lot of speculation. There is nothing substantial in the way of evidence.

But the true believer is rarely discouraged, and never wrong. He can always fall back on the ultimate argument: "You can't prove it didn't happen that way." Well, of course you can't. What are you supposed to say, "You can't prove it did"? Where does that get you? The true believer can be comforted in the thought that the dispute came off in a tie and his argument is just as good as yours.

The proper reply is "You can't prove a negative." It is the duty of the person who has the idea to present evidence in its favor, not just point out flaws in the opposing view.

If you ever find yourself falling back on a "you can't prove it didn't happen" sort of an argument, watch out. The view you are defending is very probably wrong; at the least, you are not up on the evidence to support your views and had better take another look.

THE VALUE OF BEING WRONG

These five maneuvers are a powerful part of the mental defense system that keeps us from realizing and admitting when we are wrong. As you can see, they present a major danger to effective thinking because not only do they keep us from changing our minds about a particular subject, they block and distort other channels of thought. In order to keep from being wrong we try to ignore and deny many realities. The more ideas we must defend by these methods, the more distorted our view of reality becomes.

The most foolish, and sometimes the most dangerous, people in the world are those who will never admit that they are wrong, or those who say it but don't really believe it.

RE: THINKING

Strong opinions and self-confidence are fine—but if that's all you have you won't think, you will only react. A certain amount of internal questioning and self-doubt, and above all the ability to say that you were wrong, and mean it, are absolutely essential for anyone who wants to be an effective thinker.

Fear of being wrong is one of the great killers of productive thought. If you are afraid of being wrong you will find it hard to entertain new ideas, because they might turn out to be wrong. It is like having a fear of getting lost that prevents you from going anywhere new.

The fear of being wrong can infect your entire thinking process and severely restrict your mental options. Edward de Bono says, "The very essence of vertical thinking is that one must be right at each step. This is absolutely fundamental to the nature of vertical thinking." In lateral thinking, "one does not have to be right at each step provided the conclusion is right. It is like building a bridge. The parts do not have to be self-supporting at every stage but when the last part is fitted into place the bridge suddenly becomes self-supporting."

De Bono insists, "There are times when it may be necessary to be wrong in order to be right at the end."

So don't be afraid to be wrong.

That's advice worth repeating: *Don't be afraid to be wrong.*

6

Nine Thinking Traps (and How to Avoid Them)

Let's face it, thinking is a hard and disagreeable business sometimes. It can shake up a lot of comfy old ideas. And it takes time—too much time. You can't learn everything about everything. So, like everybody else, you take some thinking shortcuts. That's OK if you're careful. If you're not careful you will fall into some traps, and they can lead you to false and destructive conclusions and actions.

I have selected nine thinking traps—they are by no means the only ones, but they are common, and I'm sure you will be familiar with all of them. Perhaps you have met one or two of them already today.

When something is classified and given a name it is easier to recognize. Read this list and study the examples carefully, for once you recognize these traps for what they are, you are far less likely to fall into them.

1.

THE OVERGENERALIZATION TRAP

One of the logician's favorite jokes is "All generalizations are false, including this one." Logic isn't a particularly humorous field, but this joke has a point, for while all generalizations are not false, and some are necessary to thinking, because we cannot examine every case in every instance, the tendency to overgeneralize is extremely seductive.

"All Irishmen are drunkards." That's an example of an overgeneralization. You may pick your own ethnic group and your own favorite vice. What is truly insidious about such generalizations is that once you have them stuck in your head, once they become a part of the pattern of your brain, they are very hard to change. Meeting with one or even several teetotaling Irishmen will not affect the basic belief very much.

Let's see how this works on a more personal and domestic level: "Every time I turn around you have spent more money" or "Every time I turn around that kid's in trouble again." Now that's the way it may feel, but it's strictly generalization. How many times do you turn around in a day? Total up how many times money has been spent or the kid has been in trouble and see. You will probably find that your generalization is in reality an exaggeration, and one that keeps you from taking a realistic look at the problem.

Generalizations of all kinds are popular in the news. They help to simplify, if not clarify, an event. A generalization can be turned into a headline, or a 30-second TV spot, but it is not necessarily informative.

A particularly doleful form of overgeneralizing occurs when the media—and here the major newsmagazines are particularly guilty—spot a new wave or mood in the country. This can cover anything from politics to popular music, from religion to high fashion. The evidence generally consists of a few statistics and a handful of interviews. Such pieces, one suspects, are less honest, if mistaken, generalizations than just journalistic gimmicks. It is instructive to save some of those "new mood" or "new wave" articles and reread them a year or so later.

While you are living through a historical period it is impossible to know whether what you are witnessing represents a major change or simply an insignificant ripple.

You can't entirely avoid generalizing in your own thinking. You certainly can't avoid generalizations every time you talk to someone, turn on a TV news program, or open your morning newspaper. But you can avoid being taken in by them.

Keep this in mind: A generalization is only a tool or device. Don't treat generalizations as if they were hard facts.

2.

THE UNTRUE TRUISM

Here is a debater's aphorism: "Even a truism is true sometimes." But, one might add, not very often.

Every time you hear, see, or think a phrase like "Everybody knows" or "It goes without saying" or "Every intelligent person knows [and if you don't too bad for you, dummy]" or "It's only too clear," be on your guard. This sort of thinking has been described as "proceeding from an unwarranted assumption to a foregone conclusion."

Here we are being asked, or we are asking ourselves, to take something for granted without examining or sometimes even being aware of the facts. These self-evident truths generally fall into two categories. The first includes homey old aphorisms like "There is no such thing as a free lunch" and "Leave well enough alone."

The other main category is the flat-out prejudice: "I believe it so, therefore it has to be true." "Everybody knows" that they (fill in your favorite racial, national, or religious group) are lazy, stupid, sneaky, dishonest, oversexed, or whatever. Everybody knows that all bankers are heartless, used car salesmen are crooked, doctors play golf on Wednesday, and suburban housewives are sleeping with the milkman. "We all know about her," followed by a wink and a jab with the elbow.

I'm quite sure that you will find that everybody knows something quite dishonorable about you, whoever you are and whatever you do. Remember that if you are tempted to slip into the habit of thinking in self-evident truths.

It is also instructive to recall many of yesterday's self-evident truths that turned out to be dead wrong. At one time everybody knew that women can't run a marathon and that Russia and China were part of the same international Communist conspiracy.

Yes, I know the Declaration of Independence begins with a statement of self-evident truths. But I submit that is a pardonable piece of political rhetoric on the part of the Founding Fathers. I doubt very much if George III found those truths to be self-evident. And unfortunately, even today a large part of the world does not consider those excellent sentiments to be self-evident truths.

It is probably pointless to ask anyone to abandon the use of self-evident truths in thinking. After all, we cannot examine every proposition that comes before us. But when you are trying to be rational, you must keep in mind that a lot of those things "everybody knows" are wrong.

3.
REVOLVING DOOR REASONING

I have spent a good part of my journalistic career investigating the subject of UFOs. I have often been confronted with an argument that in the end boils down to something like this:

"Why do you think UFOs are real?"

"Because the evidence for them is so good."

"What is this good evidence?"

"Most people believe that UFOs are real."

Stated baldly that sounds too obvious, but it is astonishing how many times a high level of interest in UFOs, or anything else, for that matter, is cited as the ultimate proof of the correctness of the belief. The Romans had a name for this: *circulus in probando*, "a circle in proof," arguing in circles.

A discussion of religion with a fundamentalist can be a perfect exercise in circular arguing. If the fundamentalist states that his beliefs are a matter of faith, that is a position to be respected and there can be no argument. But if a rational argument is embarked upon it comes out sounding like this:

"Why must the Bible be interpreted literally?"

"Because it is the infallible inspired word of God."

"How do you know that?"

"Because it says so in the Bible."

A lot of human relationships can get caught in the deadly circle.

A mother will say, "You don't appreciate me anymore. You never invite me over to your house."

RE: THINKING

"Mom, why don't you come over this weekend?"

"No, I don't want to force you to do anything you don't really want to do."

You are trapped. There is no rational exit from that circle. In both cases the conclusion is used to prove the argument.

Another form of circle is the mutual admiration society. You can often see it in operation on celebrity TV talk shows.

"Gee, Leslie, that was a great song!"

"Thank you, Ricky. I loved your latest picture."

"I think both of you are terrific. It's a pleasure to have you on the show."

"Gee, thanks, Johnny, this is a terrific show. I just love being here."

"Me too, it's just great."

This little exercise goes beyond common politeness. It is an attempt to convince you, the viewer, that you have just witnessed a group of talented people in action. There are mutual admiration societies for actors, authors, politicians, and lots of others.

We may be sophisticated enough to ignore that sort of circle, but a more insidious form of mutual admiration society exists among writers and scholars, some quite reputable. A like-minded group—we can call them X, Y, and Z—will continually quote one another as references. X confirms Y, who cites Z as his authority. Facts, if any, can get lost in the shuffle.

4.

THE TWO SIDES OF EVERY
QUESTION TRAP

A moment ago we were discussing truisms. Here is another one: "There are two sides to every question." But that depends on the question. If it's "Heads or tails?", yes, it is a two-sided question. Most questions are not so simple, though we tend to make them that way. Besides, even a coin can sometimes land on edge.

Here is one of those areas in which the problem may be due in part to the structure of our language. Some linguists believe that all of the large family of languages known as Indo-European—and that includes English and most other modern European languages—invite thinking in opposites. We look at things as good versus bad, clean versus dirty, life versus death, love versus hate, and so forth. Since the use of opposites is deeply embedded in our language, and thus in our thinking, it takes a conscious and vigorous effort to break out of the trap. People who think in other languages take for granted statements that we consider absurd or meaningless. For example, the Chinese say things like "The hard and the easy are mutually complementary." Do you know what that means? I don't. I don't think that way.

Thinking in diametric opposites is not only part of our language, it is part of our value system. "If you're not for us you're against us." "Am I right or wrong?" "Is it yes or no?" "It's moral or immoral." "All or nothing." Decisiveness, coming down hard on one side of the question or the other, is considered a virtue. To reserve judgment, to try to weigh all sides of a question, is considered indecisive, even cowardly or dishonest. "Don't be a fence-sitter," we are told. That's why sports analogies are so popular. You win or you lose; you score or you don't. However, the real world does not necessarily operate like a football game, and Vince Lombardi may not be the best model for rational thought.

In basic science many of these apparently hard-and-fast dichotomies are breaking down—where is the boundary between living and nonliving, between plant and animal, between matter and energy, between particle and wave? A century ago it would have been easy to draw the line, but no longer. Eventually this change in basic scientific thinking may change everyday thinking, but it hasn't happened yet.

The problems are not academic ones, either. When does human life begin? When does it end? Science can provide us with no unambiguous answers to those questions, and this leaves us with some of the more agonizing moral dilemmas of our time.

While we recognize that not all questions are black-or-white, we must also avoid falling into the "truth is always in the middle" trap. This is a favorite of television commentators, who, after reviewing both sides of a controversial issue, will say or imply that the truth is somewhere in the middle. Sometimes it is, for many issues are extremely complicated and both sides hold some beliefs that are true and some that are false. Sometimes, however, what seems to be two sides of a question are really two sides of different questions.

In the controversy over the cost of public welfare programs, the conservative asserts that there is a great deal of fraud and waste in such programs, while the liberal contends that there are a large number of poor people who are going to be hurt by benefit cuts. Both statements are true, but they did not address the same part of the issue. If they did and everything was either black or white, the conservative would have to say that no one will be hurt by the cuts while the

liberal would be forced to insist that the programs have op-
erated with complete honesty and efficiency. In this case
both statements would be false.

It's all too easy to assert that a problem is either black
or white (and therefore I don't have to consider any al-
ternatives) or that the truth is to be found in the middle.
But both of these formulas represent thinking traps. They
allow us to slide into an easy conclusion, one that we probably
already agreed with anyway.

There also tends to be a lot of confusion in this area of
thinking. Most disputes don't really involve "the truth."
What is at issue are different points of view or different
interests. This is true of labor negotiations, political disputes,
and most family arguments. In such cases an adequate middle
ground compromise can be worked out.

But both the black-or-white and middle-ground traps
make workable compromise more difficult. If it's either black
or white, then you feel you can't compromise, because no
compromise is possible. If the middle ground is always the
best then both sides tend to be pushed to extremes in the
hope that when the resolution finally comes it will be closer
to what they really wanted in the first place.

The recent strike of air traffic controllers provides a depressing example of what can happen when these extremes
of thinking dominate a situation.

5.
THE "AND YOU'RE ONE TOO"
EXCUSE

Perhaps you've done something like this. I know I have.
You drive into the city and park your car illegally. It's just
for a minute, you say. An hour later you come out—and

there it is, a big fat parking ticket stuck under the windshield wiper.

"What the hell is this," you think. "Why are they giving me a parking ticket with all of those violent criminals running around!"

There is a Latin phrase to describe that little thinking trap: *tu quoque*, "you also." What it means is "I did something wrong, but so did you. What are you bothering me for?"

When confronted with something unpleasant, your mind launches an immediate, if irrelevant, counterattack. Sure there are a lot of violent criminals running around, but what does that have to do with the fact that you are illegally parked? It's irrelevant, beside the point.

Back in the 1940s a stock comic phrase was "Your mother wears army shoes." It sounds incomprehensible and stupid today, but at the time it seemed hilarious. There would be an argument that would go back and forth. It could be about anything. The clincher would come when the comic hurled the phrase "Your mother wears army shoes" at his opponent. The humor came from the utter incongruity of the statement. What does Mother's strange footwear have to do with the subject? It was entirely beside the point. But people realized that, like most humor, this was only an exaggeration of normal behavior.

More often than we would like to admit, discussions don't get much beyond the "your mother wears army shoes" level. Across the river from the town in which I live there is a manufacturing plant that occasionally gives off the most foul, disgusting, and illegal odors. This has been going on for years. There are company denials, promises of cleanups, and assertions that the problem didn't exist in the first place and has now been solved. But nothing ever seems to change.

Not long ago there was a whole series of angry letters

about the odors in the local paper. Finally someone, perhaps a plant employee, responded that people shouldn't worry about the smell so long as there were so many young punks roaming around town. The letter writer was more worried about the punks than about the odors—and indeed, the punks may represent a more serious problem. But the argument is entirely beside the point. The existence of the punks did not make the odors any easier to take, nor would the elimination of the odors bring about any increase in the number of young punks on the street. One has as much to do with the other as your mother's army shoes do.

One defender of the war in Vietnam declared that he didn't know what people were so upset about since more Americans were being killed in auto accidents than in the war. True enough, but also beside the point.

This sort of defense crops up constantly in personal relations. Jim, after faithfully promising his wife that he would be at home for their son's birthday party, scheduled a business trip for that day. In the ensuing argument his wife berated him with his thoughtlessness. Very much on the defensive, Jim angrily reminded her that early in their marriage she had had a brief affair with a local artist. And off they went into a horrendous fight.

Now, personal disputes are never models of rational argument, and they are not meant to be. There is usually a good deal more involved than the problem on the surface. But if you want to keep an argument from blowing up into something much more serious, it's vital to stick to the matter at hand. In his attempt to defend himself Jim had opened an old and painful wound. You can win an argument that way, but at great cost. At most he might have said, "Look, I made a thoughtless mistake. We all make mistakes sometimes. I'll try not to do it again. Please forgive me."

This is a tough one to fight. By the time you're in this

particular trap you are already on the defensive. You're trying to protect yourself. But don't give in to this line of defense. Don't make the dispute any larger or more personal.

It is far, far easier to admit that you were wrong than
it is to wind up in a situation where you are exchanging *tu
quoque* charges with someone else. That's a situation in which
everybody loses.

6.
THE FALSE ANALOGY TRAP

You hear some delightfully juicy gossip about some
neighbors. He has been coming home very late every night.
There have been a lot of liquor bottles in the trash, and she
has been seen shopping in the morning looking red-eyed and
vague. Their children have been having problems in school.
"There is no doubt about it," your informant tells you.
"Their marriage is on the rocks, and she has started drinking."
Trying to be kind, you say that conclusion is all based on
rumors and inconclusive evidence. "Ah," you are told, "where
there's smoke there's fire." The smoke-and-fire analogy is one
of the most popular in the human mental equipment, but
only one.

Reasoning from analogy is common, and sometimes it
can be useful. Scientists use analogies all the time. But in
science an analogy is simply a model or a tool—it is not proof
of anything. The best it can do is attempt to bring the unknown or the unfamiliar into the realm of ordinary experience. Unfortunately, in popular thinking we often infer far
more from analogies than we should. We see the similarities
in the analogy and ignore all the differences. Analogies become a convenient method of allowing people to believe

what they want to believe anyway, without the necessity of proof.

Our nosy and rather nasty informant wanted to believe the family down the block was going to hell, so he pieced together a few scraps of information and tied it all together with the smoke-and-fire analogy.

Reasoning from analogy is an extremely ancient form of thinking. Things are similar in one way, therefore they must be similar in all ways. It is the basis of primitive magical thinking. The magician sticks pins in a doll made up to look like the intended victim. The doll looks like the victim, therefore it must somehow be the same as the victim, and hurting the doll will cause pain in the victim.

That sort of thinking dominated the human race for thousands of years. At one time doctors treated brain injuries with powdered walnut, because the wrinkled meat of a walnut looked like the convoluted human brain.

Usually the first hint we get of a fire is smoke, therefore if we see a hint of something it must mean there is a great deal more that we have not yet seen. "Where there's smoke there's fire." It makes sense, in a primitive sort of way. But it does not necessarily reflect reality.

There are a lot of other popular analogies: "The leopard can't change its spots." "If it walks like a duck and quacks like a duck, it must be a duck." "Birds of a feather flock together." If you think about such analogies for a moment you realize they are really silly. What do your neighbors' personal habits have to do with smoke and fire? What do leopards and ducks and other birds have to do with most of the subjects they are carelessly compared to? In most cases such analogies throw more light on the state of mind of the person who uses them than they do on the subject that is being discussed.

Analogies are also extremely popular in politics. There they serve the same purpose that they do in personal discussion—they allow someone to make a point without offering any proof to support it. Political rhetoric fairly bristles with Munich and Vietnam analogies. Any compromise will bring about "another Munich," while any military move will surely lead to "another Vietnam." Just remember that in politics the analogy is generally just a rhetorical device for expressing approval or disapproval of a particular course of action. It tells us only what the framer of the analogy thinks—it adds no information to the discussion.

7.

THE CAUSE AND EFFECT TRAP

Killing turkeys causes winter.

Every November a lot of turkeys are killed. Shortly thereafter the weather gets colder, it begins to snow, and we have winter. Since the killing of the turkeys precedes the coming of winter, killing turkeys causes winter: Cause and effect.

The example, while deliberately absurd, is a perfect representative of one of the most common of all errors in thinking, the *post hoc* mistake. The full Latin name for the error is *post hoc, ergo propter hoc*, which means "after this, therefore because of this"; because one thing follows another, the earlier thing caused the later. Another way of putting it is "reasoning from effect to cause." We see what happens, therefore assume that the thing which preceded it was the cause. Winter comes; therefore the killing of turkeys, which preceded it, caused winter.

Sometimes the reasoning from effect to cause is fairly straightforward and accurate. You are skating and fall on your arm. You are rushed to the hospital, where it is discovered that your arm is broken. The reasonable assumption is that the fall caused your broken arm.

In another example the relationship is not so clear. One winter day you are out walking without boots. Your feet get wet and chilled. A week later you come down with a severe cold. Did the wet feet cause your cold? A century ago that was the accepted medical opinion. Even today it is impossible to convince most mothers that wet feet do not cause colds. Yet there have been literally hundreds of scientific tests of this theory, and they have been uniformly negative. Wet feet do not cause colds. Think of all the times you got wet feet without suffering from a cold.

There is a bit of magical thinking going on here as well. Cold wet feet cause us to shiver and feel miserable. A cold also causes us to shiver and feel miserable. Hence one must be related to the other, and the *post hoc* is strengthened.

Let's try another example. A group of teachers are sitting around discussing their students. They get to little Michael, who is a poor student and one of the class troublemakers. "Ah, well," says one of the teachers. "His parents are divorced. He's never had a very stable home life, that's why he is so difficult in school."

That may be true, but the teacher can't prove it. There may be six other students in the class, excellent students, whose parents are also divorced, and the worst troublemaker in the room may be the child of an exceptionally stable marriage.

One of the reasons that *post hoc* thinking is so popular is that the causes of many events are not at all apparent, and this form of thought helps to fill the vacuum. Since there are generally plenty of possible causes around, we tend to pick the one that most appeals to our basic ideas. Listen to liberal and conservative economists reasoning backward to explain the cause of inflation. You begin to wonder if all these people, who are all learned in their profession, inhabit the same world.

Another reason for the popularity of this kind of thinking is that it is simple and direct. The causes of many things in the world are complex and ill understood. With one bold stroke of *post hoc* reasoning we can explain it all. That may make everybody feel a bit better, but it does not add to the general store of human knowledge, and it doesn't provide a very accurate guide to the future.

8.
THE WORLD'S FOREMOST AUTHORITY

To some degree we must all rely on authorities—doctors, auto mechanics, plumbers, lawyers, stockbrokers, movie critics—anybody who has an area of expertise in a field that we come in contact with. We don't know it all, and anyone who thinks that he does is headed for big trouble. But on the other hand, we can't allow the word of an authority to freeze all critical judgment.

The appeal to authority is an ancient one. Indeed, throughout much of history and in many parts of the world today one is not encouraged or even allowed to make independent judgments. In our own personal lives we grow up with authority. "Mother and Father know best," "The teacher says so," and so on. Some people never get over it. They simply switch their allegiance from one authority to another, for there is always someone around who is quite willing to tell you what to think. Since thinking is hard and uncomfortable work, turning it all over to someone else is much easier.

NINE THINKING TRAPS (AND HOW TO AVOID THEM)

But most of us grow out of that stage, and are thrust into a world where there are a host of conflicting authorities, all telling us different things. There are no hard-and-fast rules for choosing between them. Perhaps the best one can do is remember that they can't all be right but they can all be wrong.

At one time people put a lot of faith in ancient authorities, the older the better—somehow it seemed that the older an authority was the closer he was to some wellspring of eternal truth. This tendency has diminished somewhat in the modern world with its desire for "the latest information," but it has not disappeared entirely. (The latest information may not be any better.)

George Washington, Benjamin Franklin, and Thomas Jefferson are quoted as authorities by all sorts of people on all sorts of subjects. All of these men, great as they undoubtedly were, were still just men, not seers. They lived and wrote in the eighteenth century, in an America vastly different from the America of today. We have no idea what they would have thought today. To apply their thoughts to today's problems takes a great deal of interpretation. And that's the problem. It is all too easy to interpret an authority in line with what one already believes. You are not getting the original authority but the authority as interpreted by some later authority with his own ax to grind.

Sometimes material is presented with all the trappings of authority in order to impress. I have read a number of books festooned with footnotes to give them an appearance of scholarly authority. But when the footnotes are read they turn out to be nonsense: references to nonexistent or unavailable works, quotes from the author's own previous works, or other equally unreliable sources. It may look authoritative, but it isn't.

The long Watergate affair provided a depressing number

of instances in which material was presented with the trappings of authority and very little substance. One of the more striking examples was when President Richard Nixon went on television to announce that he was releasing the transcripts of his taped conversations. He pointed to a table piled high with bound volumes and insisted that he was making the fullest possible disclosure of his conversations. It was a very impressive-looking pile, but when the transcripts were released to the public they could be boiled down to a single book. The pile of books on TV was strictly for show. Besides, the transcripts as released had been heavily edited. All the incriminating parts were left out.

Beware of any "authoritative" presentation that tries to awe you with sheer bulk.

9.
THE FALSE EXTRAPOLATION
SNARE

You often hear people say, "Give them an inch and they'll take a mile." The Arabs have an expression about the "camel's nose under the tent." It's the desert version of the "give them an inch" argument—just let that camel get its nose under the tent and pretty soon you'll have the whole camel in bed with you. Another way of putting it is reference to the "thin entering wedge." If this little thing happens all these presumably horrible consequences will follow.

This kind of thinking is based on extrapolation, or more simply prediction. You take a little bit of information, mix in a lot of preconceived notions, and come out with a big guess. Except you don't call it a guess; it's stated as an absolute certainty.

Like all of the other thinking traps we have been discussing, this one is highly seductive. You can't prove all those terrible things won't happen, and you don't have to consider a lot of complicated possibilities. If this happens, then that will surely happen, and that's it!

Scientists use extrapolation all the time, but not until they have mustered a significant array of facts and can justify the extrapolation. Even then they make it clear that what they say is an extrapolation, and not a divine prophecy. In politics and personal life we are not so scrupulous.

"If you let the child get away with that she'll never listen to you again."

"If one of *them* moves in the whole neighborhood will be overrun in a year."

Or, the grandest of them all, "If things keep going as they are the whole world is going to be destroyed for sure."

The best way to protect yourself against falling into this particular thinking trap is to remember all of the great predictions of the past that fell flat. When I feel I'm falling into this trap I think of Quemoy and Matsu.

Do you remember Quemoy and Matsu? If you're over forty you may—though vaguely. Quemoy and Matsu are a couple of barren islands off the coast of China. Back in the mid-1950s we were told that if the Communist Chinese took control of Quemoy and Matsu they would quickly overrun Taiwan (or Formosa, as we called it then) and the rest of Asia, and would soon threaten the United States itself. This is not an exaggeration. This is what a lot of people said and thought in the mid-'50s. The two islands were a major campaign issue.

What happened? Quemoy and Matsu were ultimately taken over by the Communist Chinese. But by that time they had ceased to be an issue. Taiwan is still there. The Chinese have not overrun the rest of Asia. They are not menacing San Francisco. Indeed, they have become our allies of sorts.

RE: THINKING

The great Quemoy and Matsu prediction was absolutely wrong. Unfortunately, people don't remember wrong predictions.

Keep that one in mind, because false extrapolations always get a good workout during election campaigns.

You should also ponder these words of wisdom from Stuart Chase, the author of *The Tyranny of Words* and *Guides to Thinking Straight:* "Thin entering wedges can and do split great rocks. But the process is not inevitable for all rocks, or for all types of wedges."

You can also remember the "fatal glass of beer." At one time people were told, one drink and that was it. You were on a one-way trip to alcoholism and skid row. Now, alcoholism was and is still a serious problem. But the "fatal glass of beer"? Hardly.

What this trap does is cloud the issue and make thinking more difficult.

7

How Not to Get Snowed

ARISTOTLE CAN HELP YOU

Every day, practically every hour of our waking lives we are bombarded by appeals: Buy this. Do that. Vote for X. Vote for Y. Believe this. Believe that.

There is so much that you are probably tempted to try to turn it all off. Or simply not believe anything you hear. But that's not wise, or possible.

There must be some way to separate the hokum, the nonsense, and the propaganda from what is real and important.

Fear not, help is available—and from a very unlikely source, too, the ancient Greek philosopher Aristotle. Aristotle was the founder of the practice called "formal logic." I'm going to show you how to apply some of the rules of logic to modern situations.

Don't let that scare you. A lot of people become nervous when they hear about the "rules of logic." They think it must be like calculus or other forms of higher mathematics, and will be quite beyond their comprehension. Logic also has a reputation for being "cold" and inhuman. We fear that our own thought processes are hopelessly flabby and illogical, and that our cherished beliefs will crumble in the face of a "logical argument."

It's no accident that the popular modern symbol of the logical thinker is *Star Trek*'s Mr. Spock, a being allegedly without emotions and not truly human. We may feel like running when the specter of logic is raised. We become poor Dr. McCoy shouting ineffectually at the icy but logical Spock.

But basically logic isn't that strange or hard to understand. The ancient Greeks, just like ourselves, were faced with a lot of people who tried to force ideas on them. Just like ourselves, they wanted to separate the fact from the nonsense. So Aristotle worked out some rules to help them do this.

THE LOGIC GAME

Logic began as a game. The Greeks were great game players. They were particularly fond of a word game that might be called the "yes or no" game, which had two players and a question. It didn't really matter much what the question was, just so long as it could be answered by a simple yes or no. One of the players took the yes side, the other the no side. One of the players asked questions of the other, questions that could be answered either yes or no. The aim of the questioner was to cleverly phrase a series of questions to force his opponent to admit that he was on the wrong side. If the questioner managed to trap his opponent into such an

HOW NOT TO GET SNOWED

admission, then he won the game. If the opponent avoided such an admission, then *he* won the game. The truth or falsity of the proposition was not the issue.

When Aristotle came down to study at the famous Academy in Athens he was shocked at the way the game was being played. It didn't seem to have any rules. If a game doesn't have any rules then anything is possible, so Aristotle decided to write a book of rules for the game, to help players recognize the nonsense. Ultimately he wrote several books of rules. The rules of this game are the basis of formal logic. That's it. Forget anything else you may have heard about logic being a way to find "the truth" or anything else. It's a game. Logic can help you from being snowed, but you shouldn't be snowed by logic.

Once you fully realize and appreciate the fact that the logicians of ancient Greece were primarily game players, out to score points against their opponents, you will be able to see how Aristotle's rules of logic can be useful in helping us think today.

The logicians of old knew how to use all manner of tricky and downright fraudulent arguments. And they knew how to spot them as well. If logic can't provide a royal road to "the truth," it can at least help keep us from being bamboozled by all the old gamester's tricks—for there are only a limited number of tricks. The great nineteenth-century philosopher Schopenhauer wrote, "I realized that regardless of persons or topics of discussion the same tricks and dodges recurred again and again and could be easily recognized." The same tricks and dodges are still with us, and with a bit of help we can still recognize them.

Today most of us don't have to be worried about being beaten in a game by a slippery-tongued philosopher. We face the old tricks and dodges primarily in two areas, advertising and politics. These are two areas in which others are trying to force us to a foregone conclusion—that we must buy Brand X or vote for Candidate Y, support (or oppose) Proposition Z.

EIGHT COMMON FALLACIES

These tricks are commonly called "fallacies." Aristotle compiled a list of the most common ones. Aristotle spoke and wrote in Greek, but most of his works have come down to us in Latin translation, and the Latin adds a certain air of weighty authority to the list of *argumenta* ("arguments, proofs, or appeals to reason"):

argumentum ad hominem, "to the man"
argumentum ad populum, "to the masses"
argumentum ad misericordiam, "to compassion
    (or pity)"
argumentum ad baculum, "to the club"
argumentum ad crumenam, "to the purse"
argumentum ad verecundiam, "to modesty"
argumentum ad ignorantiam, "to ignorance"
argumentum ad captandum vulgus, "to please the
    crowd"

Don't worry if you have forgotten your Latin (or never knew any); these popular fallacies are not nearly as formidable as they sound. Indeed, they are quite commonsensical, and it's reassuring to know that the ancient Greeks relied on common sense just as we do (or as we try to do). But it is depressing to see that people have been using the same tricks to try and put one over on others for so many centuries— and unless you have been well warned in advance, the old tricks still work.

Here then is a little ancient Aristotelian advice on how

you can keep from being snowed by the corporations with their advertising agencies and the politicians and their expensive media consultants.

1. The *argumentum ad hominem* is an appeal to personal prejudices and has nothing whatever to do with the question under discussion.

Have you ever noticed how, during an election campaign, nearly every candidate is described as "a good family man" (except, of course, if they are women)? There are endless pictures of the candidate with the wife and kiddies, and even the family dog. Does the candidate really have such a wonderful family life? Does it make any difference anyway? The candidate is not running to be your neighbor, or a member of your family. At the time, who but a relatively small group of insiders knew that Franklin Roosevelt and John F. Kennedy had rotten marriages? Did that somehow make them unfit to be president? By all accounts Herbert Hoover had an excellent family relationship; did that make him a better president? There are more important issues on which to judge a candidate, but if you saw some political advertising you wouldn't think so.

In our more sophisticated age, the old "family man" appeal has taken on new forms from time to time. In Ed Koch's first campaign for mayor of New York City, he (or his media consultants) apparently decided that the voters would have a negative reaction to his lifelong-bachelor status, so he contrived to appear regularly with Bess Myerson, a former Miss America and a Koch political associate. They were photographed holding hands, and there were even rumors (coyly denied) that marriage was in the offing. After Koch won the election Myerson suddenly disappeared from his side. She reappeared only at ritual party functions, like any other political associate.

On the other side of the country, California's Governor

RE: THINKING

Jerry Brown, seemingly afflicted with the same sort of worries over bachelorhood, suddenly appeared regularly in the company of popular rock star Linda Ronstadt. In this case too there were hints of impending marriage. Linda Ronstadt faded from the scene at about the time Governor Brown abandoned his attempt to get the Democratic party's nomination for president.

All this is what might be called the positive side of the *ad hominem* argument; the negative side is good old-fashioned name-calling. Name-calling was once a fine art in American politics. Unhampered by strict libel laws, nineteenth-century politicians regularly accused one another of being thieves, liars, drunks, and generally disreputable and undesirable individuals. Today this sort of charge is floated more discreetly, and often by individuals not directly connected with the candidate. Name-calling persists but it has gone underground. Since name-calling has gotten a bad name, one of the most common ploys is for one candidate to accuse another of name-calling or mudslinging, even when none has taken place. That is its own form of name-calling.

It isn't just politicians who engage in cutting one another up instead of arguing matters of substance. It takes place in the highest academic circles, just as it does in the streets and wards of the city. It's an amusing, if not very edifying, spectacle to watch a couple of distinguished professors rip into each other viciously and with real personal malice, then piously accuse each other of launching *ad hominem* attacks.

The *ad hominem* fallacy can be practiced visually as well as with words. A particularly striking example are those television ads for a chain of auto transmission repair shops. All the other people who repair transmissions are shown as fat and stupid-looking, while the representative of the outfit being advertised is invariably a slim, square-jawed straight shooter. If Aristotle could have viewed these commercials he

HOW NOT TO GET SNOWED

would doubtless have muttered, "*Argumentum ad hominem*" —though he probably would have said it in Greek.

2. The *argumentum ad populum* is an appeal to mass emotions. In politics the best example is what is called the "bandwagon effect." Most politicians try to create the impression that their candidacy or policy is supported by a large and rapidly growing number of voters—therefore you had better support it too (get on the bandwagon). Another form of the fallacy is the appeal to the "mandate," which simply means "We won the last election." All of these appeals are made without reference to the value or wisdom of the candidate or policy being discussed.

Sometimes the appeal can backfire. It was reported that one particularly inept New York politician who was running for mayor stood up before a group of black ministers whose support he was seeking and botched his *ad populum* appeal with the words "My heart is as black as yours."

The old slogan "Fifty million Frenchmen can't be wrong" was the perfect *ad populum* fallacy. In product advertising all statements about the item being the "largest-selling" or "most popular" are representatives of this fallacy.

3. An appeal to pity is what is meant by *ad misericordiam*. The most celebrated example of this in modern political history was then Vice-President Richard Nixon's "Checkers speech." Accused of impropriety while serving as Vice-President under Dwight Eisenhower, Nixon responded with a weepy speech in which he talked about his dog Checkers and his wife's cloth coat. The appeal worked.

A candidate is never behind, he is always an "underdog," a position that is said to attract sympathy.

A particularly vicious and tasteless *ad misericordiam* advertising campaign was run by an insurance company. It showed two children being led away by a court officer. The aim was to implant in your mind the idea that if you didn't have enough of this company's insurance your poor children would someday become wards of the state.

4. The *argumentum ad baculum* is an appeal to force. Direct appeals to force are relatively rare in modern American politics—but veiled (and not so veiled) hints that if the other fellow is elected there will be anarchy and blood will run in the streets or Russian tanks will roll through Kansas are not unknown. The charge that Candidate X is "soft on crime" is the most frequently heard *ad baculum* appeal today.

5. *Ad crumenam* means "to the purse"—obviously an appeal to money. What politician today does not promise lower taxes without any corresponding pain? There is some brief mention of sacrifice, but usually the implication is that someone else will do most of the sacrificing, and that they (whoever they may be) can afford it anyway.

A simple and honest statement of price is not a fallacy. Advertising that claims a product costs less than other "major brands" but does not specify, and the type of automobile advertising that gives a price loudly and then quickly runs past a whole string of options (which cost extra) and other additional costs are all fallacious.

6. The *argumentum ad verecundiam* is an appeal to prestige. Under this fallacy we can list the testimonial. Is it really important that a candidate is supported by Frank Sinatra, or a particular product is supposed to be used by Reggie Jackson? Of course not. Such testimonials are crude appeals to prestige, but surprisingly effective or at least widely used ones. When Walter Cronkite retired from active news broadcasting, all sorts of advertisers were after him to endorse their products because he was supposedly "the most trusted man in America." Cronkite resisted the temptations.

7. *Argumentum ad ignorantiam* is a Latin phrase close enough to English so that you could probably figure it out yourself—it is an appeal to ignorance. The politician who

tosses a whole mass of facts and figures at his audience, information he knows they cannot understand or evaluate, is making this sort of an appeal. The advertiser who pushes some "scientific breakthrough" or "miracle ingredient," particularly if the ingredient has a long and impressive-sounding name, is appealing to the ignorance of his audience. The opposite also can be true—people can be frightened away from a product because it contains an ingredient with a long chemical name, though the chemical may be quite harmless. A generation ago a mouthwash advertiser threatened non-users with "halitosis," which is just a scary name for bad breath. Or take those "natural" cereals that are about one half sugar. Sugar is a "natural" product, so the advertising is not flat-out dishonest, but the advertiser clearly hopes that the potential buyer doesn't know that he is buying primarily fattening, tooth-rotting "natural" sugar.

8. *Argumentum ad captandum vulgus*, to catch the crowd, is a general term for any of the fallacies already mentioned and for any other dishonest or misleading arguments.

You may feel that the list and the examples that I have given you are obvious and that you would never be taken in. Well, perhaps. But encountering fallacies clearly labeled on a list and encountering them in everyday life are quite different. We are surrounded by so many people and organizations that are trying to force us to some preordained conclusion that we are sometimes battered into switching off our critical and logical faculties and simply swallowing what is tossed at us. Repetition, as everyone from Adolf Hitler to Madison Avenue has known, is extremely effective. A fallacious, even utterly ridiculous statement, if repeated often enough, is going to be believed by a lot of people—people who should know better.

Advertising men and media consultants are highly skilled, and paid very well by companies and individuals who want to force us to accept certain conclusions. And no matter how smart and sophisticated we may think we are, none of us are entirely immune to the advertiser's appeal.

At the back of all of our minds there is a little voice that says things like "They couldn't say that if it wasn't true." That statement is utterly wrong, of course, but it's a mind-set that is hard to break.

It is useful every once in a while to take Aristotle's list of fallacies and apply them to the advertising you encounter in a day, or to the political rhetoric that you hear.

CONSIDER THE SOURCE

A couple of other tips used by the logicians of old are also useful in today's world. First among them is the axiom "consider the source."

When we see an advertisement from the manufacturers of Brand X extolling the wonders of Brand X, we have a pretty good idea of what is going on. The ad does not necessarily contain lies, but it is there for a purpose, and the purpose is not to inform you but to get you to buy Brand X. Most of us automatically take that into account when evaluating product advertising. However, there are forms of advertising in which the source and motive are more difficult to locate. This is particularly true with certain types of "public service" advertisements, aimed not so much at selling a particular product or candidate as at changing public attitudes on an issue.

Generally media require that the source of advertising be identified, but often the sponsors are called something like "The Institute for Freedom and Democracy." That could be anybody, for after all, who is against freedom and democracy?

HOW NOT TO GET SNOWED

Unfortunately, considering the source can sometimes lead to a form of paranoia—distrust of anything that we don't already agree with—if we assume the source is somehow tainted. It can also cause us to overlook or dismiss potentially valuable information because we distrust the source. Even information from a biased source is not automatically wrong or invalid.

Since most of us don't have the time, interest, or facilities to check out most of the information that daily crosses our path, we must at least try to keep the source of the information in mind when evaluating it.

FEAR OF NUMBERS

Like most people, I guess that I look at numbers with a mixture of incomprehension and awe. I have quite enough trouble balancing my checkbook at the end of the month, even with the aid of an electronic calculator. When faced with rows of statistics I tend to avert my eyes.

An old college friend of mine named Roland made brilliant use of statistics. Whenever he got into an argument —which was pretty often—he always seemed to have the relevant numbers to support his case. He could quote this or that study, or the latest government statistics on whatever it was that was under discussion. His skill snowed people completely, and we all thought he was brilliant.

One day I asked him how he managed to keep all those numbers in his head. "Oh, I don't," he said. "I just make 'em up as I go along. No one ever challenges me, because they are afraid of numbers."

You bet we are. Yet there is no doubt that numbers are extremely important in our lives, and they are thrown at us daily—sometimes with the intent to deceive. People don't have to be making the figures up either; the very nature of the figures themselves can be misleading. Antony Flew makes this point in his book *Thinking Straight:*

"Suppose you boast that the New Splodge contains 50 percent more of some gorgeous ingredient. Then your boast is as near as makes no matter to completely empty if no one knows, and you are not telling, how much there was in it before."

How about those omnipresent toothpaste ads that promise 40 percent fewer cavities for your children or are supposed to get your wash 30 percent brighter? Forty percent fewer than what? Thirty percent brighter than what? Or how about those tablets that contain "40 percent more of the pain reliever that doctor's recommend most"? (That's aspirin, by the way.) Such statements are meaningless and misleading—deliberately so.

Flew continues: "No doubt true statements can be doubly misleading thanks to certain very simple mathematical properties of percentages; the birth of your second child constituted a 100 percent increase in your family, whereas if you were to have a fifth that one would represent only a 25 percent addition to your previous four; if you were to suffer a 50 percent cut in anything you would then need a 100 percent increase to get back to where you were before."

In 1981 advertising for the Chrysler Corporation boasted that the tottering company had a greater percentage of increase in sales over the past year than the big two auto manufacturers, Ford and GM. Doubtless a true statement—but misleading, since Chrysler's base of sales for the previous year had been a disaster. In absolute numbers of cars sold the figures did not sound so impressive, so they were not used.

In his book *The Art of Deception* Nicholas Capaldi shows how figures can be used by presenting the financial report of a fictional large corporation. Capaldi lists the relevant figures as follows:

Earnings:
(a) 1 percent of sales, or
(b) 1 percent on a dollar, or
(c) 12 percent on investment, or
(d) $5,000,000 profit, or
(e) 40 percent increase in profits over 1939, or
(f) 60 percent decrease in profits over last year.

All of these statements, Capaldi points out, say exactly the same thing, but the way in which they are presented give them a different look:

> A retail organization takes in a large gross, but actual net receipts after expenses are very small. The first two figures (a) and (b) reflect this fact. You may begin to wonder how in the world any corporation stays in business or would want to stay in a business for such a small profit margin. The answer is that daily sales bring in a large amount of cash which can then be invested at high interest rates for the remainder of the year. We are all familiar with the fact that the larger the amount of money you can invest, the larger the percentage of the return. The same one percent may, by the end of the year, return twelve percent. By the end of the year the actual profit in dollars may be, as in (d), $5,000,000. How does this profit compare with past performance? It all depends, again, on the frame of reference. If we choose the 1939 level as base period, profits have increased substantially. If we choose last year's profits as the frame of reference, profits may have decreased even though the company is still earning a profit.

Capaldi then goes on to give examples of how these very different views of the same information can be used. In arguing against those who say that profits are excessive and

RE: THINKING

there should be some form of price control, management would refer to (a). In talking to the stockholders management would naturally stress (c) and (d) or even (e). When contract renewals come up and a union must be negotiated with, management will stress (f). The union will counter with (d) and (e) to press its demands for higher wages and benefits. At a stockholders' meeting a group of dissidents will shout about (f) as evidence that the present board of directors is incompetent and should be replaced.

One of the most widely used (and misused) terms in statistics is *average*. We are always being told about average, but do you know what the word means? It can mean *arithmetic mean*, the total divided by the number of people or things involved. But that's only one meaning. An average can also be the point halfway between the number of people and entities involved. That's also known as the *median*. Then there's the *mode*, the point at which you find more people or entities on the scale than at any other point. So whenever you are presented with the figure for the "average" try to find out just what sort of average is being presented.

Not only that, two people can look at exactly the same set of figures and come up with completely different interpretations of what they mean. Let us say that liberal John is passionately in favor of handgun controls while conservative Dave, a member of the National Rifle Association, just as passionately opposes them. They are both shown statistics indicating a dramatic increase in gun-related crimes over the past ten years. John will see in the statistics the need for control of handguns, whereas Dave will deduce from these same figures the need for honest citizens to own guns to protect themselves from all of the armed criminals.

Which is right? The statistics, even if they are accurate, will not give you the answer.

Before you meekly accept conclusions drawn from any

HOW NOT TO GET SNOWED

set of figures, here are five questions to ask yourself. These questions are suggested by Darrell Huff, author of *How to Lie with Statistics*.

1. Who says so?
2. How does he know?
3. What's missing?
4. Did somebody change the subject—that is, shift the base or the scale for the statistics?
5. Does it make sense?

8

The ABC's of Arguing

THREE THINGS YOU CAN DO WITH AN ARGUMENT

Arguments can be one of life's plagues. They can be frustrating and agonizingly gut-wrenching. But they don't have to be that way. There are three things you can do with an argument. You can avoid it. You can win it. You can lose it. The trick is to know why, when, and how to do each. Once you know, you can escape the pain of arguing, and you can profit from some arguments.

Most people don't really know what is going on during an argument. They just plunge right in, and they get burned, sometimes badly.

Let's look at a typical argument.

Jake and Harry are good friends, but their political views are very different. Jake is a political liberal from way back. The first vote he ever cast in a presidential election was for Adlai Stevenson. Harry is a devout conservative who voted for Barry Goldwater and was an early supporter of Ronald Reagan.

Most of the time Jake and Harry don't talk about politics, because politics is not a central part of their friendship. But one day they start a little discussion. Two rational, intelligent adults—surely they should be able to discuss a subject calmly, without excess emotion.

But it doesn't happen that way. Very soon the discussion has escalated into a full-scale shouting match. By the time the argument is over both men are red-faced and extremely angry. Each is convinced the other is an idiot or worse. Both spend a sleepless night refighting the argument in their heads.

The following day both look up some things in their favorite books, in order to prove that they are right. They also consult with like-minded friends, who assure each of them that he is completely correct and his opponent doesn't know his facts and used all sorts of unfair debater's tricks.

Within a few days Jake's liberal ideas and Harry's conservative ideas are more firmly entrenched and stoutly defended than ever. And their friendship has been badly damaged.

What is the most significant thing that happened (or rather, didn't happen) in this example? Both men became upset. A friendship suffered as a result. *But nobody's mind was changed.* In fact, the argument had the exact opposite effect.

Nobody won. Everybody lost. It was one of those arguments that should have been avoided. Jake and Harry didn't avoid it because they didn't understand the way our minds work during an argument. If you understand what's going on you will be able to step away from many of those pointless and potentially damaging arguments.

Our memories and beliefs are stored in our brains in the form of nerve cell patterns. When you argue with someone

RE: THINKING

you are pitting your nerve cell patterns against his. The beliefs and opinions you hold are not the result of some abstract intellectual process. They are the result of your total life experience. But your opponent's beliefs and opinions are the same. For both of you, changing these deeply held beliefs is hard and painful.

Since we all want to avoid pain, we all want to avoid changing these beliefs and opinions. The mind will work very hard to defend them.

If an argument isn't a means of persuading people, what is it? It's a fight, an attack, and you react to it as such. Your heart pounds more rapidly and your face gets red, just as it does during physical exertion like fighting. Your muscles tense, the adrenaline rushes into your bloodstream, your blood pressure rises. All the basic body changes that are present during a physical fight are there during an argument.

Imagine you are trying to get someone to try a new breakfast cereal. You are not going to grab him by the shirt-front and try to force a spoonful of the cereal down his throat. If you did the person would probably spit it right back in your face. But that's what happens during an argument. You are trying to force something on someone. He will spit it right back at you. Even if it's good for him and tastes good, he won't accept it. Neither would you.

You now can see why probably the vast majority of arguments can and should be avoided. They don't change anything, and they never will. The techniques for actually persuading people to change their minds are much different from the direct attack involved in arguing. Getting a person to change his mind is a slow and often devious procedure.

HOW TO WALK AWAY FROM IT

Avoid arguing. That's easier said than done, because some very basic mental and physical processes are involved. Like every other animal, human beings possess what is called the fight-or-flight reaction. When we feel threatened, our bodies gear up to fight or, if fighting is impossible, to run away. Any argument is a threat. That's why even small disagreements can blow up into major arguments that quickly turn personal and nasty. Once we get ready to fight, the process becomes self-perpetuating. So we have to try to stop it before it really gets started and becomes much harder to control.

You should think of an argument the same way you think of some sort of minor physical intrusion, because that's the way your body and your unconscious mind react to it.

Let's say you are walking down the street and someone bumps into you. What do you do? First, you may think, "It's my fault," and say, "I'm sorry," to the other person. Or you may think it's the other person's error, and still say, "I'm sorry," just to be polite.

In rare cases you may feel the other person deliberately bumped into you. What do you do then? Are you going to turn around and jump the guy? Of course not. What's the point of getting into a fight in the middle of the street? Besides, the other guy might be bigger and beat the hell out of you. So nine out of ten times you swallow your anger and just walk away. Don't be ashamed. It's the right thing to do.

At one time people didn't do that sort of thing. Every insult, real or imagined, had to be avenged. There were duels and vendettas as a matter of honor. People killed one another over tiny insults. But all civilized societies have worked hard to suppress this sort of activity. We can get along very well without it.

Kids in the schoolyard will still bump one another and issue challenges. "Ya wanna make something of it?" But as adults we outgrow that behavior.

Of course, if someone actually attacks you on the street then you have to respond. You either fight or run. But the start of most arguments is more like a bump. You don't absolutely have to react. You can walk away, and nine out of ten times you should.

There is no shame in saying: "I don't think we should discuss that." Or: "I have a different opinion, but let's not go into it now." Or simply: "It's pointless to argue about this subject. Let's talk about something else."

FOURTEEN TIPS FOR WINNING ARGUMENTS

Sometimes arguments cannot be avoided. Sometimes they should not be avoided. Let's say there is someone who is constantly trying to provoke you by saying in your presence things that are deliberately hostile and obnoxious. Or you may know someone who is spouting a lot of nonsense to other people who are believing him. Then you might have to get into an argument.

If you find you have to argue in a situation like this, you may as well argue to win. Winning an argument can be fun. But before you get into any argument you must remember that an argument is a fight, not an intellectual exercise. You are almost certainly not going to persuade your opponent of anything. He will probably hate you even more when the argument is over. Also remember that an argument isn't a search for the truth. Indeed, the truth is usually obscured in the process.

Winning can be a dirty business.

With all that in mind, here are fourteen tips that you can use to help you win practically any argument.

1. Stay calm, or at least appear so even if you don't feel that way. If you look as if you are in control it makes everything you say appear more rational, even if it's not. If your opponent loses his temper, so much the better—you can then accuse him of being hysterical or irrational. If he betrays real feeling about a subject, look sympathetic but insist that decisions cannot be made on an "emotional basis."

2. While uncontrolled anger is usually harmful to a case, a well-directed show of anger can be effective. One of the best practitioners of the use of controlled anger is New York's Mayor Edward Koch, a uniquely effective politician. When asked an uncomfortable or hostile question, he will often respond with a show of indignation and shout that he will not be intimidated and pushed around. Not only does he appear to be standing firm and put his questioner on the defensive, he is able to avoid answering the question at all. A show of effective anger may also allow you to insist that certain charges are "unworthy of being answered" when in reality you just can't answer them.

3. Be sure of your facts when you are specific, particularly if you suspect that your opponent knows something about the subject. Being caught in even a trivial error of fact, one that does not affect the main thrust of your argument, can be very damaging, for it makes it appear that you don't know what you're talking about. It also allows your opponent to spend time talking about your error rather than the subject. If you think you might be tripped up, stick to generalities. And of course, be on the lookout for an error

RE: THINKING

in fact, no matter how trivial, in your opponent's argument.

4. If you can't spot any error in your opponent's facts, and if they appear to be damaging, ask him to cite his sources. Most of the time people don't remember where they got their information, and if they do you can always try to discredit the source.

A member of a school board that had banned a number of books was being attacked, and one of the arguments used against him was that several of the banned books were Pulitzer Prize winners. The school board member immediately responded by recalling the recent scandal over the awarding of a Pulitzer Prize in journalism to a false story. The Pulitzer Prize was thus neatly discredited.

5. If you feel an argument slipping away from you, ask your opponent to "define your terms," then attack the definitions. Since very few words have exact definitions, there is almost always something to attack. What does *freedom* mean? The right to vote? Freedom from want? The right to trial by jury? Freedom for whom? The possibilities are endless. At the very least this definition game will delay the argument and confuse the issue, and perhaps give you time to recoup.

6. Use the all-or-nothing technique—extend your opponent's argument to the "logical extreme," even if it isn't logical. Every point has an absurd, not a logical, extreme.

7. Always claim your opponent has misstated your case, whether he has done so or not, because it gives you a chance to imply that your opponent has misunderstood what you are saying and is stupid, or has deliberately twisted your words and is dishonest. This is akin to the "straw man" ploy. You say your opponent has set up a straw man, or false argument, that he can knock down. Then show how your own argument differs from the straw man. At this point you can set up your own straw man.

THE ABC'S OF ARGUING

8. If you are trapped in a misstatement, insist that your words have been taken out of context, or that your opponent is ignoring the "spirit" or "principal thrust" of what you have said.

9. If you are accused of inconsistency, deny it. If you really have been inconsistent and have been caught at it, it may be possible to reinterpret your previous statements to bring them in line with what you have just said. And if all else fails you can fall back on the proverb about consistency being the hobgoblin of small minds. Your opponent may not accept that very graciously, but it's better than admitting you are wrong, particularly if you can carry it off with flair.

10. Red herrings are extremely useful, especially if things are not going very well. "Remember," says Nicholas Capaldi, "the only thing that always sticks to a point is a dead insect on display." Search around for some side issue on which you feel particularly strong and try to divert the argument in that direction.

In a discussion on the policy of apartheid a South African white was being attacked for his country's racial policies. He replied, "Why are you people always attacking us? We are the only stable anti-Communist nation in Southern Africa. Why don't you worry about those Cuban troops in Angola?" That may be a valid point, but it is also a red herring when the subject under discussion is South Africa's racial policies.

11. Damning the alternative is another useful technique. If you have offered a proposition, don't let your opponent simply attack you—make him offer an alternative. If he can't, claim that you have won the argument by default. If he does offer an alternative, attack it.

Let us say the argument is over capital punishment. The person who favors capital punishment, after being attacked on moral, sociological, and legal grounds, responds by saying, "All right, we have all these murderers walking the streets,

now what would you do about it? What's your alternative?"
Any reply to that challenge is likely to be a diffuse one that
does not have a satisfactory sound.

12. If your position seems very weak, you can always try
to justify it by insisting that it is necessary because of the
errors or the evil deeds of the opposition. On the political
level it might be something like "Our side is justified in
committing atrocities because the other side commits atrocities." On a personal level it can be "Yes, I acted badly—
because you drove me to it."

13. And there is always the flat-out personal attack. You
say your opponent is an idiot, a louse, or the tool of some
sinister force. Then close down the argument by saying you
never argue with such people. That is a rather dangerous
maneuver, akin to kicking over the board in a game of chess,
and it opens you up to all kinds of charges of bad faith.
Still, it may be better than a flat-out loss.

14. If you are convinced that you are a firm winner in
the argument, be gracious. Don't go for total victory by
nailing down every point. In the first place, the longer you
argue the more chance your opponent has of coming up
with an effective argument; thus, you are putting your
victory in peril the longer you go on.

Appearing gracious also makes a good impression on the
audience, if any. It is not generally wise to humiliate your
opponent, even if it is possible. He probably dislikes you
quite enough already; there is no need to make it worse. And
if you do have some genuine interest in persuading him,
rather than besting him, it is best to leave some of his dignity
intact, or he will never listen to you.

A TIE IS BETTER THAN A LOSS

But, as the old saying goes, you can't win 'em all. And there are still a number of things you can do when you see your argument going down to defeat. Rule number one is, never admit that you were wrong. You may admit the necessity for modifying your position somewhat, or at the very worst you can say that while some of the details of the argument were weak, the basic underlying principle, "which is the important thing anyway," is correct.

You can also declare yourself a winner by definition. In an argument over the possible legalization of marijuana you can state flatly, "Drugs are evil." What sort of argument can there be for legalizing evil? You win by definition. That sort of arbitrary declaration is not going to gain you a great deal of admiration except among those who already support your point of view, but you may feel it allows you to escape defeat.

Perhaps the most effective method for escaping from an unsatisfactory argument relatively unscathed is to go for a tie and declare that you and your opponent, who is a nice fellow, are really in basic agreement. In doing this you must appear friendly, and as if you are genuinely concerned and sympathetic to his position, no matter how deeply you disagree on minor details. You may even be able to get away with saying that you are glad your opponent has come over to your point of view. The technique may sound absurd, but I assure you it can work.

Not long ago I witnessed a debate between two politicians on environmental issues. They held diametrically opposing views on virtually everything. Yet as the end of the debate neared one of the two (the one who in my opinion had been coming off poorly in the argument) beamed broadly and said that he was so glad that he and his opponent were in basic agreement with the underlying principles of protecting the environment without harming the economy. His opponent sat in stunned and embarrassed silence.

In practically any argument you should be able to find some suitably broad and bland principle upon which you can claim agreement. If your opponent persists in pressing the disagreements he runs the risk of appearing to be the bad guy, while you are genuinely trying to be a healer.

And if all else fails, declare that the question is not yet settled and more investigation (or thought or time) is needed. The tobacco industry has been successfully using the call for more research for years.

WHERE IS THE TRUTH?

All of this may sound quite cynical and Machiavellian. And it is. But, as I have repeatedly stressed, arguments are rarely successful in persuading another to your point of view. Even less are they a search for truth. Most arguments are fights, and not fights governed by the Marquis of Queensbery rules either. They are street fights with no rules.

Here I have listed only some of the intellectual devices that can be used in arguing. This is not the place to go into the many emotional elements, the crying, the appeals for pity, the threats, and so forth that make up such an important part of most arguments, particularly personal arguments.

Think back over the arguments you have had, or those you have heard, from arguments conducted over the dinner table to presidental "debates." How many of the techniques that have been outlined here have been used? How many minds have truly been changed by the content of the arguments?

If you wish to improve your skills in arguing, try this little exercise suggested by Nicholas Capaldi. Chose a controversial subject about which you hold a strong opinion, something like abortion or the legalization of marijuana. Now try to construct an argument *against* the position that you hold. Don't cheat. Make the argument against your own opinion as good as it can possibly be.

Not only does this exercise give you a chance to sharpen your skills in arguing, you may learn something.

HOW TO LOSE AND STILL WIN

As I said at the beginning of this chapter, there are three things you can do in an argument: walk away from it, win, or lose. Losing may be the most valuable technique of all. You don't have to win every argument you get into.

Let's start with an obvious example. You are having an argument with your boss over the relative merits of baseball and football. You're an old sandlot baseball player, while your boss was first-string varsity halfback in college.

You can muster a lot of arguments on your side. You can point out to him that football is an extremely dangerous sport. You can tell him how you think big-time college football debases many college academic programs. You can tell him you find football boring. You can tell him a lot of things. But what's the point? You will never change his mind.

But it's not an argument that you can walk away from. Football is his passion and he loves to talk about it. You can't tell him, "I don't want to discuss it."

You might be able to win the argument. But then your boss would be mad at you.

The best thing to do is lose. "You know, you might be right. I never knew all of that. Maybe I don't understand the game too well. Next time I see a football game I'll remember what you told me."

Your boss walks away with a warm feeling toward you. You have suffered no loss of dignity. And—wonders of wonders—once you relaxed and decided not to contest every point, you might have been able to really listen to what your boss was saying, and you learned something new about football.

OK, that's an easy one. Learning how to lose well in most domestic arguments is more difficult, and more important.

WHAT'S THE ARGUMENT
REALLY ABOUT?

Larry and Janet had just been married. She was a girl from a small town. He was a New York City boy. Because Larry got a good job in New York, they moved to the city. Janet managed to find a receptionist's job but was hoping for something better.

They were shopping around for furniture for their apartment when Janet picked out a chair she said would look great in the living room. Larry thought the chair was a horror. He pointed out all of the things he thought were wrong with it. It was too big. It was the wrong color. Its shape was ungraceful. It wouldn't go with anything else.

Janet tried to counter all of his points. He was adamant. So was she. Then quite suddenly she burst into tears and began screaming at him, right in the middle of the store. It was an ugly scene.

Larry was shocked because he didn't know what the

argument was really about. He thought Janet was arguing about chairs. She was really arguing about her self-worth. She had moved into Larry's city, adopted Larry's style of life, and bent her own aspirations to Larry's career. Now she felt she was being told she didn't even know what kind of chair to get.

Most domestic arguments are fought on two levels, and the hidden one is usually the more important.

Larry should have lost this one. "It's a little unusual, but I see your point. It might look great. We'll try it."

By losing the argument both Janet and Larry really would have won. He would be showing confidence in her judgment, and that would help her reestablish her self-esteem. That's the important part. If he won, all he would be winning was an argument about a chair. Besides, she might really be right—the chair might look great.

THINK BEFORE YOU ARGUE

Next time an argument presents itself, run through these basic points.

1. I'm not going to change anybody's mind, and I'm probably not going to learn anything.
2. Can I walk away from this one?
3. If I win, what will I win, and what do I stand to lose?
4. If I lose, what do I lose, and what do I stand to gain?
5. Do I know what we are really arguing about?

9

Five Steps to Stop Fooling Yourself

WHY LEO KEEPS SMOKING

How much time and mental energy do you spend convincing yourself that it's really all right to do things that you know you shouldn't do? If you are an average person, the answer to that question is plenty—too much.

The process is called "rationalization." It's natural, normal, and we all do it sometimes. The reason we do it is simple—we want to avoid mental pain. In previous chapters we have seen how the mind, like the body, reacts automatically when threatened with possible pain.

Here's what happens. Doing something that we know we should not do creates a state of mental confusion, and genuine pain. It is a state that psychologists call "cognitive dissonance." At the same time, we hold two ideas (cognitions) that are diametrically opposed to each other. This creates conflict, or dissonance. And that is a painful state of mind that we try to avoid.

Automatically we try to reduce or eliminate the pain by convincing ourselves that what was done was really all right. The reaction is as automatic as flinching if you think that you are about to be hit. It's a natural, even necessary reaction. We can't go through life agonizing over every wrong thing we do—we would be immobilized. But, like so many other useful mental processes, rationalization can go too far. It can seriously distort our thinking and our view of reality. Sometimes it can lead to disastrous consequences.

But the process of rationalization can be channeled and controlled.

First let's see how it works. Take the case of Leo.

Leo smokes. Like most people, he is well aware of the overwhelming scientific evidence indicating that smoking causes lung cancer and contributes to a host of other deadly and debilitating diseases. Yet Leo continues to smoke, and if you ask him why he gives you a number of different answers.

"I don't really smoke so much anymore. The risk is really high only for heavy smokers. Besides, I smoke low-tar cigarettes."

"When I tried to stop smoking I gained a lot of weight. Being fat is worse for your health than smoking."

"Nobody in my family ever died of cancer. My father smoked and he lived to be seventy-three. People who get cancer come from cancer-prone families."

"These scientific studies really don't mean much. According to the studies practically anything you do causes cancer."

"When I smoke it cuts down on my emotional stress. Stress is the thing that really kills you."

"I really enjoy smoking. You have to die from something. Look at poor old Jim. He didn't smoke, he didn't drink, he ran five miles a day, and then he got hit by a truck. If your number is up, then your number is up."

All of us, smokers and nonsmokers alike, will recognize this line of thought. Leo is trying to justify something that he is doing, that he knows perfectly well he should not be doing. He is not a liar, or a particularly self-deceptive person. He is simply trying to protect himself from pain. He has made the statements so many times he almost believes them.

Leo the smoker is in a state of cognitive dissonance, holding two diametrically opposed ideas: Smoking is bad for me; I am a smoker.

Leo needs to reduce the pain. In his case there would be two possible ways of doing this, either stop smoking or convince himself that smoking is not so bad after all. Since he does not believe he can stop smoking, he has embarked on the latter method of making his mind more comfortable: He rationalizes.

Leo's family and friends have often argued with him on the subject of smoking. They have pointed out how self-serving and irrational his excuses are. Leo tries to turn these arguments aside, and if the other person persists, he becomes angry. "It's my life, I'll do what I want with it."

When his wife gets after him about his smoking he thinks, "She's always nagging me. She makes me so nervous, that's one of the reasons I smoke." Thus, he has even come to blame his habit on a person who is trying to make him stop smoking.

FIVE STEPS TO STOP FOOLING YOURSELF

1.
RECOGNIZE THAT YOU ARE HUMAN

Leo's problem is a common one. There are millions of smokers who try to convince themselves that what they are doing is really not so bad after all. In cases such as these the rationalizing is helping to prolong a potentially dangerous habit. But just preaching isn't going to help. As Leo's wife found out, it may make things worse.

As anyone who has ever tried to break the habit knows well, smoking is a tenacious behavior pattern. There are all sorts of systems and techniques to help the smoker kick the habit. None of them are magic. Giving up smoking is a hard thing to do.

Before the smoker gets far enough to try a "cure," he first has to stop kidding himself. He has to stop rationalizing. He has to face up to the reality of the problem. This is a necessary preliminary in the cures for all addiction. And in order to face up to the problem he must lower the pain caused by the cognitive dissonance. There are five steps that can be taken to do this.

Here is the first: Recognize that, like all other human beings, you have a strong tendency to defend yourself and avoid mental pain by insisting that you are right. In short, realize that it's perfectly human to rationalize.

If you don't recognize that rationalizing is a normal, indeed inevitable human activity, you are going to find yourself in a double bind. You not only have to defend the original activity, you have to defend your defense. That increases the cognitive dissonance, the mental pain, and the need to rationalize it away. This makes a solution to the problem even more difficult.

2.

WE ALL ACT BADLY—SOMETIMES

Step number two can be illustrated by reference to some of the most controversial psychological studies of modern times. The studies involved getting volunteers to subject others to pain, either psychological or physical.

Usually the pain was not real, because the supposed victim knew what was going on and was not psychologically distressed, or the electric shocks that the "torturers" thought were being administered actually were not. But the torturers in these experiments did not know the pain was not real. A lot of people objected to these experiments because they were cruel. However, it is not unreasonable to speculate that at least some of the objections were raised because the conclusions were so disturbing that they had to be rejected somehow.

Psychologists Keith David and Edward Jones designed an experiment in which student volunteers were supposed to listen in on an interview. They were then to tell the person being interviewed some very negative and even cruel things about himself. The psychologists found that the students' opinion of the object of their cruelty declined after they believed they had hurt him. Instead of feeling sorry for him, they managed to convince themselves that to some degree he *deserved* it.

In another experiment, conducted by Ellen Berscheid and her associates, student volunteers were supposed to deliver painful electric shocks to other volunteers. Half the group was told that there would be a turnabout in the experiment and later the victims would have a chance to deliver the same sort of shocks to their torturers.

The study showed that those volunteers who thought that they would not receive any shocks and their victims were essentially helpless had a far greater need to justify their actions by derogating their victims than did the students who thought they would be shocked in return. The belief that they too would be shocked tended to greatly reduce the mental pain. "We'll both get electric shocks so we will be even." Inflicting pain on helpless victims required a far greater effort of self-justification. The harm-doers in the experiment had a greater need to convince themselves that somehow the victims deserved it.

Psychologist Elliot Aronson of the University of Texas, author of *The Social Animal*, suspects that this sort of mental process operates during wartime. Otherwise decent individuals are forced into a position where they must commit acts that under peacetime conditions would be considered criminal or inhuman. The soldier is able to justify his acts by convincing himself that the enemy deserved it, that they are evil or somehow less than human. It also helps account for a phenomenon sometimes noted in wars, of respect for the enemy soldier. He can kill you, therefore the thought of killing him does not create so much mental anguish; it does not need to be justified by finding him less than human.

Most of us think of ourselves as decent, moral human beings. But, like the torturers in the experiments, or soldiers in warfare, we sometimes find ourselves in a position where we do or are forced to do things that we consider immoral, stupid, even cruel and criminal. The act conflicts with our view of ourselves. Result: cognitive dissonance, pain, and a rapid retreat into self-justification.

But once again, self-justification or rationalization can make the problem worse. The soldier who has managed to convince himself that the enemy is less than human or has somehow deserved it is much more likely to commit acts even worse than what the situation requires.

In less dramatic circumstances we may cheat on a test, or do something cruel and insensitive to a friend. If we start justifying these acts ("Everybody cheats" or "He's just a jerk anyway") we are not going to be better off, we are going to be worse off.

So here's step number two: Recognize that just because we have done something that is stupid and/or immoral, that does not necessarily mean we are stupid and immoral people. In short, try to isolate the act, get it in prospective, not in order to justify it, but to reduce the need to justify it.

3.
YOU ARE WHAT YOU
THINK YOU ARE

This leads directly to step number three. People who think of themselves as good and decent suffer from a lot of cognitive dissonance when they do something they consider wrong. But not everyone thinks of himself as being good and decent. A lot of people have a very low self-esteem. What happens when a person who has low self-esteem does something that should be considered wrong?

Says Dr. Aronson, "Theoretically, if he were to commit a stupid or an immoral action he would not experience much dissonance. His cognition 'I have done an immoral thing' is *consonant* with his cognition 'I am a schlunk.' In short, a person who believes himself to be a schlunk expects to do schlunky things. Another way of putting it is that a person who has low self-esteem will not find it terribly difficult to

FIVE STEPS TO STOP FOOLING YOURSELF

commit an immoral action—because committing an immoral action is not dissonant with his self-concept. On the other hand, if a person has high self-esteem, he is more likely to resist the temptation to commit an immoral action, because to behave immorally would produce a great deal of dissonance."

That's the theory anyway. It was tested in a study conducted in the 1970s by Aronson and David Mettee.

A group of students were given what they were told was a personality test. After the test one third of the students were told good things about themselves—for example, that the test showed they were mature, interesting, and so forth. Another third were given negative results—immature, uninteresting, etc. The final third were given no test results at all.

Immediately afterward the same students took part in another test, which they were told had nothing to do with the first. This second test involved gambling for money. During the course of the test the students were presented with several opportunities to cheat in situations where it seemed they could not be detected. Of course, they didn't know that the chance to cheat was built into the test; they just thought they had a chance to get away with something. If they cheated they stood to win a fair amount of money. If they did not cheat they would lose a fair amount.

The students who had just been told they were rather worthless individuals tended to cheat to a far greater extent than the students who had been told how good they were. Those who had been told nothing were right in the middle.

Aronson believes that the implications of this study may be quite far-reaching, particularly for parents and teachers. If low self-esteem contributes to dishonest or cruel behavior, "then we might want to do everything possible to help individuals learn to respect and love themselves."

So that's step number three: Increase your self-esteem, and you will be less likely to do stupid and immoral things.

4.

WHAT'S DONE IS DONE

In a charming novel titled *The Private Life of Helen of Troy* John Erskine has his character Helen explain her philosophy that one should repent only in advance. After something is done there is no point in repenting, she says.

But our minds do not work that way. The more committed we are to something, the more we need to justify it. Unlike the fictional Helen, we cannot simply accept things as they are. We may not repent, but we certainly do try to justify.

Here is an example of how that works. A psychologist posing as a market researcher showed a group of women several different kitchen appliances—a toaster, an electric coffeemaker, and the like. The women were then asked to rate the items, and as a reward would be given a choice of one of the two items that they rated as most attractive.

A few minutes after the choice was made, the women were again asked to rate the items. This time they rated the item they had chosen somewhat higher and the item they had decided against somewhat lower than before. They had made their choice and they were now in the process of justifying it. They had to think that the item they had chosen was better than the item they had rejected.

Once a decision is firmly made the need to justify it becomes stronger than ever. Psychologists went to the racetrack and questioned bettors on their way to the two-dollar window. These bettors were only reasonably sure that the

FIVE STEPS TO STOP FOOLING YOURSELF

horse they were going to back would win. But those bettors who had already placed their bets expressed a far higher degree of confidence. They had made an irrevocable decision and were in the process of convincing themselves, and the world around them, that it was the correct one.

That makes life more comfortable. But it also distorts our perception of reality. So step number four: Do your thinking beforehand. It's much better than trying to justify your decision afterward.

5.
WE ALL MAKE MISTAKES

And finally, in the light of our mind's natural tendency to justify itself it is necessary to repeat a point that may seem obvious, but that some people don't seem able to accept —we all make mistakes. We are always going to do some things that are stupid, cruel, or just plain wrong. And our minds will quickly (and very effectively) spring into action in an attempt to justify what we have done or failed to do, by saying that it wasn't stupid, cruel, or wrong. There is little point in telling ourselves either not to make mistakes or never to try to justify them. That sort of behavior is part of the human condition. It's like telling yourself not to flinch when fingers come toward your eyes.

However, the person who spends too much time protecting his ego has a problem. I suppose we have all met the kind of person who apparently has never done anything wrong but is put upon by the world. Whenever something is amiss it is someone else's fault.

Sometime the condition is temporary. Typically, after a divorce both parties will tell their friends how horrible the other one was, and how correct *they* were to do whatever it was they did. The experience of separation is a painful one. The self-justification helps to reduce the pain and rebuild a damaged ego. In time the parties may be able to look at the situation more coolly, and the need to justify every act and derogate the other person will no longer be so strong.

Then there are those who will never be able to change. As Elliot Aronson points out: "The autobiographical memoirs of former presidents are full of the kind of self-serving, self-justifying statements that can best be summarized as 'if I had it all to do over again, I would not change a thing.' "

It would be best for us to be able to recognize and admit our mistakes, stupidities, and cruelties, and try to learn from what we did wrong so that we will not find ourselves in the same position again.

THE FIVE BASIC STEPS

As we have seen, self-justification is inevitable, but when carried on to excess it distorts our view of reality, and can result in some unfortunate and even disastrous consequences. So let's go over the five basic steps for cutting down on the need for self-justification.

1. Understand that, like all human beings, you have a strong tendency to defend yourself and to believe that you are right even when you are wrong. Then you won't have to justify your justifications.

2. Understand that just because you have done something that is stupid and/or immoral that does not necessarily mean you are completely stupid and immoral. Then you won't have to justify everything you do.

3. Build a good self-image. That will make it more diffi-

FIVE STEPS TO STOP FOOLING YOURSELF

cult for you to do things you consider wrong, and will also allow you to tolerate your errors.

4. Recognize that what's done is done. Do your thinking beforehand and you won't have to do so much justifying afterward.

5. Recognize that, like everyone else, you make mistakes, and that it is necessary and useful to admit that you do.

10

How to Avoid Word Trouble

WHAT'S IN A NAME

A lot of the problems that you encounter in thinking are caused by a confusion of words. No, not getting one word mixed up with another (though that causes trouble too)— the main source of trouble is getting the word confused with a thing.

When, early in life, I first heard the phrase "the word is not the thing," it seemed an obvious enough statement. But after a few years I realized that it wasn't obvious at all. We all spend a lot of time confusing words and things. As a result, we get into a lot of trouble and waste a great deal of time in frustrating and unproductive thought.

In some ways, I suppose, the confusion is natural. Words are extremely important to us. We communicate by means of words. We think in words. The use of language is one of the characteristics that makes us uniquely human.

HOW TO AVOID WORD TROUBLE

Ancient peoples recognized the importance of words, and that is where the confusion began. To many ancient people words *were* things. People had secret names, known only to themselves and to the priest or family member who gave it to them. For everyday use they had an everyday name, but it wasn't "real" or important.

Why a secret name? Because the name—the word—was believed to be part of the person. It had a power of its own. If the name became commonly known that would dissipate the power. Besides, the name might come into the possession of an enemy. Then, since the name itself was a thing, and part of a person, it would give the enemy power over the person. Remember the old fairy tale of Rumplestiltskin? The maiden had to obey the dwarf until she found out his secret name. As soon as she did, he lost his power. The roots of that story go back a long way.

To the ancient Hebrews the name of God was so awesome and powerful it could never be spoken aloud. It was to be whispered only by the chief priest on the holiest day of the year in the most sacred part of the inner sanctuary of the temple of Jerusalem.

Many ancient people believed in "magic words"—words that when spoken in the proper sequence would accomplish certain desired ends. Today there are still those who try to ban all books, including dictionaries, that contain "dirty words," as though a word itself had a magical power to corrupt.

IS "GOODNESS" SOLID?

The Greek philosophers rejected this simple type of word magic, but their own ideas about words we might find peculiar today. Plato and his followers taught that things like goodness and truth were not abstract qualities but actual things. They apparently believed that somewhere out there existed a real essence or entity of "goodness" or "virtue." True, no one had ever seen it or felt it, but that did not make it one bit less real.

Ultimately the speculations of Plato and his followers became wedded to religion. The result was a powerful system of thought that dominated the Western world. For over a thousand years long and complicated arguments were conducted over abstractions like *goodness* and *virtue*. Throughout the Middle Ages these arguments were carried out primarily by monks who were cloistered and cut off from the world around them. To their way of thinking, the abstractions represented the true and important "reality," while the material world was transient and unimportant, and at best a pale reflection of these "higher realities." All problems, they felt, could be adequately solved by speculation and proper reasoning, for that was the only path to "truth." All the equipment for solving any problem already existed in a person's mind and soul. All you had to do was think hard enough. Facts were quite irrelevant. The *word* had become more important than the *thing*.

The medieval thinkers were very serious about this. They wrote long treatises on various subjects that we would consider quite absurd today. The old joke about speculation over how many angels could dance on the head of a pin was not too far off the mark. If you got on the wrong side of one of these arguments you might find yourself in an uncomfortable, even dangerous position. Books and sometimes their authors were burned for pursuing an argument that was deemed by the authorities to be incorrect. Since there was only one truth, and anyone could find it by proper thought, to arrive at some other conclusion was not only wrong, it was heresy, and that was a burning offense.

HOW TO AVOID WORD TROUBLE

Not much of this speculation had held sway beyond the walls of the cloister. Out there in the world of peasants and merchants and soldiers people didn't worry much about abstract qualities. They were too concerned with the material things that kept them alive: when to plant crops, how to test the strength of a sword or the purity of a piece of gold. Such people were constantly up against the material world, and it was reflected in their plain homey language. They didn't confuse words and things. But then, they weren't considered, and did not consider themselves, thinkers.

Slowly the world in which it was important to observe what was happening and the world of thought and speculation began to draw together. Sometimes this caused confusion and conflict. For example, by pure reason the thinkers had constructed a perfect view of the universe, with the earth in the center and the sun the moon and all of the planets and stars revolving about it in perfect circles.

Scripture supported by reason told them that the earth was the center of the universe. The circle was a perfect figure, and as the universe created by a perfect God could be nothing less than perfect, everything had to move around the earth in circles. It is a beautiful mental construction and it made excellent sense, so long as you didn't look up in the heavens to see what was going on. The observations of the actual movements of the stars and planets conflicted with this perfectly reasoned mental picture.

Nicolaus Copernicus, the astronomer who first figured out that in order to bring theory in line with observation it was necessary to conclude that the earth revolved around the sun, realized the radical nature of his approach. Not until he was dying did he allow his ideas to be published. He did not want to die any sooner than was necessary.

Galileo, who championed Copernicus's ideas, got into serious trouble with the Church. There is the famous story of

Galileo's opponents refusing to look through his telescope. This is often cited as a perfect example of pigheaded medieval stupidity. But that characterization isn't really fair, for it fails to take into account the way Galileo's opponents thought—the way most educated and intelligent people in Europe had thought for over a thousand years. As far as they were concerned, the nature of the universe had been set down in Scripture and elaborated by pure reason. The result was a beautiful and perfect universe that reflected the perfection of God. What could be seen through Galileo's ridiculous gadget was unimportant and perhaps dangerously misleading when measured against the two powerful springs of truth, revelation and pure reason.

Ultimately, of course, Galileo's way of perceiving reality won out, at least in the realm of science. And it has become a standard ideal for almost all forms of thinking: Don't get caught up in abstractions. Try to test the thought, the word, against observable reality. That's why somewhere along the line most of us have been reminded that "the word is not the thing."

Today most of us would agree that qualities like "goodness" are abstractions, which exist only in our minds. We view events and people, and think some of them good, some not so good, and others downright bad. There are enormous areas of disagreement. Consider, for instance, the differing images in people's minds of Ronald Reagan, and the resulting estimates of his "goodness."

There is a whole school of wise men and women who advise us to be as concrete as possible in our thinking, to rely on what we can see and measure, rather than on abstractions and generalities, in making decisions and drawing conclusions. That sounds like pretty good advice. The trouble is that many of the most important things that we think about in life seem to involve just the sort of generalities and abstractions we are told to avoid.

SOME HARD QUESTIONS

In the middle of a sleepness night, or while sitting at the seashore or staring idly out a window, some hard but abstract questions tend to pop into our minds. They are things like:

"What is the meaning of life?"

"What is my place in the grand scheme of things?"

If you're not feeling too cheerful: "What's the point of it all?"

Or, on a somewhat less cosmic level: "Does he/she really love me?"

There are two schools of thought about such questions. The practical thinkers, of whom we have just been speaking, hold that they are questions composed of meaningless abstract words, and thus are of no importance at all. The other school holds that such deep questions are the only important ones and are therefore the most useful to ask.

The medieval scholars attacked just such questions. Armed with their training in formal logic, they were able to build magnificent theoretical edifices—which sounded wonderful but didn't connect with the real world. Lacking the medieval scholastic's skills in formal logic, we can't construct any theoretical edifices and tend to simply brood unprofitably over such questions.

So practical thinkers are correct and they are useless questions, right? No, not exactly, and we can't banish them from our thoughts. They are always coming into our minds at inappropriate moments. Such big questions are inevitable, and we have to be able to deal with them.

RE: THINKING

Here are some tips:

1. Recognize that such questions are abstractions. They represent general feelings or emotions, but not physical things. They cannot be dealt with in any manner that we would normally consider rational or logical, so don't try. You can't think through the answer to any of life's big questions.

2. Try to reduce the cosmic questions to a more concrete level, one that can be dealt with in concrete terms. Rudolf Flesch, author of *The Art of Clear Thinking*, suggests that instead of asking, "What is the meaning of life?" you ask, "What did I do today and for what purpose?" Instead of trying to find your place in the grand scheme of things, try to define your place in your family, your company, your community. Granted, even the reduced questions are not all that easy to answer for most of us, for they too involve some abstraction, but they do give the rational side of our minds something that it can begin to deal with effectively.

3. These questions can arise at dark times in your life— three in the morning of a sleepless and anxiety-filled night. The only possible answers you can come up with at such a moment are gloomy. Tell yourself that you should not be trying to deal with global matters at such a moment, and thinking about them will only make you feel worse. You will not always feel the way you do at that moment. Things will look different and better in the morning. As best you can, simply try to avoid the big questions at such moments. You might try the technique suggested in Chapter 12.

4. On some bright, blue-skied mornings the meaning of life seems clear and it's good to be alive. You know that it all makes sense and that you have an essential place in the cosmic scheme of things. You even know "she loves me." Of course, such thoughts are no more real than the dark night feelings, so don't try to reason them through. Such moments

are among the high points of life—just stand back and enjoy them.

PUTTING IT INTO WORDS

If we can't put the answers to the big questions into words, we can put practically everything else into them. And the words that we use really do influence the way we think. The word may not be the thing, but the mind does not usually make that distinction. Indeed, the relationship between language and thought is so intimate and complicated that philosophers and scientists have scratched their heads (and scratched at one another's eyes) over the problem for centuries. Get a dozen language theorists together and you will probably get a dozen wildly different ideas about the interrelationship between language and thought. One of the primary arguments is over whether the nature of a language determines what a person can and therefore will think, or whether the method of thought determines how a language will be formed.

Every language—and there are about two thousand different ones spoken in the world today—is complete, complex, and in every way comparable to other languages. There are no truly "primitive" languages. The Bushmen of South Africa, the aborigines of Australia, and all of the other peoples who are usually classed as "primitive" have their own fully developed languages. "There is no more striking general fact about language than its universality," wrote anthropologist Edward Sapir. The grunts and shrieks that are sometimes used to represent primitive languages in the movies are crude distortions.

But if everybody has a fully developed language, it does

not mean all languages work in the same way. In all languages there are certain words that cannot be translated into other languages. I grew up in a household with a Yiddish-speaking grandmother, and I found that there are many words that cannot be adequately translated into English. *Chutzpah*, for example, might be translated as having gall, or brass or balls, but not quite. So in many places *chutzpah* has been adopted into English, because it has no good equivalent but is quite a useful word. So is the Yiddish word *shlump*—a jerk, a drip, a loser—yes, but not quite. You know a shlump when you meet one, even if you can't give him a name in English.

WHEN A ROSE IS NOT A ROSE

A rose is a rose is a rose, said the writer Gertrude Stein. A gardener might disagree. Certainly you couldn't say snow is snow is snow to an Eskimo, who wouldn't know what you were talking about. Eskimos have about a dozen different words for snow—one for drifting snow, one for falling snow, one for snow on the ground, and so forth. Eskimos spend a lot of time looking at snow, and its exact condition is of great importance, so their language makes fine distinctions. Skiers and meteorologists also have a number of different words for snow, and even children distinguish between "good packing" and "poor packing" snow. In many specialties— science, music, engineering, etc.—people are almost forced to invent their own special language, sometimes called "jargon," because the ordinary language doesn't have words to cover all the necessary concepts. The more words you have to describe things, the more precise your thinking can be. Eskimos can think very clearly about snow.

Sometimes language formation lags behind necessity. Probably the greatest gap in modern English is in the area of new personal relationships. It's ludicrous to have a forty-year-old man refer to the thirty-five-year-old woman he has been living with for six years as his "girl friend," yet it happens all the time. What other word is there? Mistress, roommate, lover, consort? None of the words are really right; they all have inappropriate connotations. Is this middle-aged man her "boy friend"? What does a child who has an affectionate relationship with his mother's third husband call him? Father? Stepfather? Fred? Are two gay men who have had a long-term relationship husband and wife? Certainly not. For that matter, are they gay or homosexual?

Other societies have languages that contain words that cover all of the subtleties of highly complex family systems. Our language is still stuck in the nuclear family era. Over the past decade we have easily adopted many of the words from computer and space technology into our everyday speech—we speak of people being "programmed" and "deprogrammed," for example—but we still talk of thirty-five-year-old "girl friends."

I suspect that this is because we are not entirely comfortable with many of the new and more open relationships that we now see. To give them a name of their own would somehow also give them a legitimacy, a permanence, that society is not ready to recognize. So we resist. Every time we think about these relationships there is a mental pause as we insert an inappropriate word. That affects the way we think.

TWO KINDS OF MEANING

Every word you speak has two layers of meaning. One is the literal or dictionary definition (denotative meaning). But words also evoke all sorts of emotional and subjective associations that are not formally stated (connotative meaning). These can be far removed from the dictionary definitions, and much more important.

Psychologist Charles Osgood measured the connotations evoked by a variety of words. Not surprisingly, he found that people from similar backgrounds found the same connotations in words. For people of differing backgrounds, however, the connotative meanings can be very different.

Consider the phrase "law and order." To a white city dweller the words may conjure up the image of the cop on the corner who will protect him from being mugged. To the black city dweller the same phrase may connote a racist legal system and the threat of vigilante action.

A few years ago a candidate for mayor of New York City had a stock speech in which he referred contemptuously to people who threw garbage into the streets. Black leaders objected, saying he was making a racial slur. The candidate vigorously denied this and insisted that he was speaking about anyone, white or black, who threw garbage into the streets. And indeed the candidate never singled out any racial group as being particularly guilty. Yet this was a speech made only in white communities. This candidate rarely, if ever, spoke in the black community. It is impossible to believe that the phrase did not conjure up in the minds of his listeners a picture of blacks throwing garbage out of tenement windows. It is also impossible to believe that the candidate did not know exactly what connotations his words had. A great deal of political rhetoric relies on "code words" of this sort.

Of course, connotative meanings are not all bad. Everyday language would be pretty barren if it were not rich in connotations. Literature and poetry would be impossible. But we pay for this richness with a loss of precision.

Scientific language attempts to avoid words with connotative meanings. When observers of animal behavior speak of a lifelong relationship between male and female greylag geese they describe it as "pair bonding," not "love." The word *love* means too many different things to too many people.

Substituting neutral words for common ones can lead to its own set of problems—the creation of jargon. Jargon can be a way of covering small thoughts with big words, or it can become a secret language, for initiates only. Only lawyers seem to know what other lawyers are talking about.

DO YOU SAY WHAT YOU MEAN?

Not only do words have two different levels of meaning, the setting, the tone of voice, and the volume of speech can all change the meaning. "Harry, you old SOB" said in a hearty voice and accompanied by a slap on the back means one thing. Growled in an undertone and accompanied by a piercing stare, it means something quite different.

You must be sensitive to these differences, for if you listen only to the words, you run a serious risk of misunderstanding others. And remember that others are going to have the same problems with what you say, so be extremely careful. It's difficult to convince someone that "I didn't really mean that the way you took it." Nor does the charge "You're being too sensitive" usually go down too well when someone feels insulted by something you have said.

If you want to avoid this kind of word trouble, think ahead. Consider not only the words you use and the meaning they have to you, but their probable affect upon others. Words not only carry a dictionary definition, they can conjure up a host of mental images far more powerful than the intended meaning.

RE: THINKING

The problem can be acute between people of different cultural backgrounds.

Karen had grown up in a strict Protestant family in Texas. It was a family in which decorum and politeness were considered of prime importance, and negative feelings were rarely expressed in words. A simple "Oh" or a furrowed brow were strong expressions of disapproval. Everyone knew what they meant.

In college she met Nick, an Italian-American who had grown up in a Chicago suburb. Since the college they attended was near Nick's home, he took her to meet his family. It was not a successful meeting. Nick's large and loud family alarmed Karen. Nick and his brother traded insults from the moment they got together. After dinner everybody got into a shouting match, and Karen was sure there was going to be a fight. She became genuinely frightened.

She tried to explain her fears to Nick. "You were saying such terrible things to one another."

"That's the way we always are," Nick responded. "We're a typical close Italian family. We fight all the time, but it doesn't mean anything. If we stopped yelling at each other it would mean we didn't care about each other anymore. Don't you understand? You can't take what we say literally."

Karen was no great success with Nick's family, either. They complained that she was stuck-up and rude, because she hardly talked to anybody. She thought she was just being polite.

Even with the best of intentions they had managed to misunderstand each other.

In a community near to where I live a tremendous fuss was kicked up not long ago over the use of the phrase "Heil Hitler" in a high school yearbook. To the editors of the yearbook and their young faculty adviser World War II and Nazis were distant history. Everyone knew who Hitler was,

HOW TO AVOID WORD TROUBLE

and he unquestionably was regarded as evil, but the mental image evoked by "Heil Hitler" did not carry any real emotional force for the young people.

It was quite different for some of the older people in the community, many of whom had fled from Nazi Germany or fought in World War II. To them it was like a slap in the face. No amount of reason could convince them that an insult had not been intended. Once again, different backgrounds produced sharply different mental images from the same words.

In politics the words that are spoken are not necessarily the best guide to the meaning. Today most Americans are fairly sophisticated, even cynical, about political language. We tend to dismiss much of what is said as "political rhetoric"—meaning just empty words, don't take it seriously.

In certain parts of the world the words used in politics are extremely violent. In the Middle East exaggerated political speechmaking is a way of life. The politics of the region are pretty fierce and violent, but if you listen to the words that are used you would think no agreements were ever possible between certain nations, or that other friendships between nations were eternal. Neither of these is true, as the history of the region proves. Exaggerated political speech is the style; they understand it. Often we fail to.

Diplomatic language is just the opposite—the rhetoric is understated. "Frank and full discussions" can be translated as "We argued like hell and didn't agree on anything."

THOUGHTS ON PAPER

While we think in words, the words that flow through our brains are not really the same as the words that we speak or write. Anybody who has ever tried to write anything, particularly fiction or poetry, knows this.

You have this marvelous idea. It seems to be well worked out in your head. Then you sit down and try to write it, and oh my! The gap between the words you have in your head and what you are able to set down on paper is so broad that the experience can be enormously frustrating. One of the most difficult things for the novice writer to get used to is that no matter what you write, it still sounds better in your head. While words may only be an approximation of reality, they are also only an approximation of your thoughts.

Each word in our head can conjure up a vast tapestry of feelings and images. The same words placed coldly on a piece of paper do not have the same impact. They certainly do not have the same impact on another person, for whom they evoke very different connotations.

Also, our minds will make or slide over all sorts of connections and ambiguities that must be filled in on paper or in speech. Sometimes the bridge between two thoughts doesn't really exist, or we are incapable of locating it. That's one of the reasons that writing out thoughts or speaking them into a tape recorder may help clarify our thinking. We are no longer allowed the luxury of skipping over parts of the thought process. We must examine our ideas more objectively to see if they make sense.

How often have you found yourself in the position of saying something like "Well, I can't exactly put it into words, but you know what I mean"?

HOW TO AVOID WORD TROUBLE

There are indeed many thoughts, feelings, and concepts that cannot adequately be put into words. Don't be put off by the rather snobbish statement that if an idea cannot be explained, it must therefore be no good. Some people are better at explaining ideas than others, and some ideas are more easily explained. Certain areas of experience and thought are quite beyond adequate explanation for most of us. A moving poem puts into words thoughts that were only half formed in our minds. Besides, a lot of nonsense can be made to sound very rational. Throughout the eighteenth century the "Age of Reason" physicians could give a perfectly rational explanation for the widespread practice of bleeding patients. There was a whole elaborate theory about balancing the "humors" of the body. As we now know, bleeding cured no one and killed many. But it sounded perfectly reasonable at the time.

What you cannot expect, however, is that other people, particularly people who do not know you well, are going to be able to read your mind. What seems to you so obvious that it hardly needs saying may be completely hidden from someone else.

That feeling of "You never listen to me," "You deliberately misunderstand me" may not be justified. Our words may trigger a particular set of connotations and associations in our own minds but quite a different set in someone else's head.

Words are only symbols of objective realities. They are also only approximations of our thoughts. Don't be too quick to assume that another's misunderstanding is due to willful stupidity. There are a lot of barriers to be overcome in communication. At best we overcome them only partially, and we should be patient and understanding when the inevitable confusion arises.

SOME FINAL WORDS

Let's round out this chapter with a summary of practical advice on avoiding word trouble.

1. Remember that the word is not the thing.

2. The big abstract question may feel important, but you will never be able to "think through" the answers, so don't waste your time trying.

3. The more precise your vocabulary is, the more precise your thinking is likely to be.

4. All words have two levels of meaning, the denotative or dictionary definition and the connotative or subjective association. When you speak to others be sure you are getting across the right meaning at both levels.

5. Writing a problem down will help clarify your thinking about it, because it forces you to examine your ideas more objectively.

6. Don't expect others to read your mind. If you want to be understood, say what you mean, as forcefully and clearly as possible.

11

When to Think (and When Not To)

ARE YOU A MORNING PERSON?

Once I had a discussion about working habits with one of America's leading writers of thriller fiction.

He told me that he would regularly wake up at four in the morning, make himself a cup of coffee, and then work until eight, when the rest of his family got up. He had breakfast with them, then he would work for several more hours. If he was under deadline pressure he would even work at night.

"But those early morning hours are the best. Between four and eight the house is quiet, and my mind seems to click right along."

Hearing this man's working habits made me shudder. I can't imagine sitting in front of a typewriter in a quiet dark house at four in the morning and producing anything.

Four A.M. is unthinkable—but mornings in general are not

RE: THINKING

good for me. I don't feel that my mind is functioning very efficiently until about 11 A.M. The period of the day in which I can do my best work, when my mind is sharpest and clearest, is between approximately 7 and 10 P.M.

These are not my work "habits"; they are more than habits. For many years I worked at a regular nine-to-five office job. Mornings were still hopeless, and had to be devoted to the most routine sort of work. Afternoons were somewhat better, but if I had something really difficult to do I took it home and finished in the evening. I didn't like to work in the evening, but I had to.

I tried to change this pattern by going to bed earlier, or later, by drinking coffee, by switching my lunch or dinner hours around. Nothing really worked. Though there might be some variation from day to day, over any extended period I was still sluggish in the morning and most awake in the early evening.

In the years since I have been a full-time writer and more or less able to make my own hours, I have still tried to alter the schedule, so that I can have a more normal evening—so that I can bring my working time in line with what everybody else is doing. I have never succeeded. If I am really serious about getting something written I will be in my office at about 7 P.M.

I am a prisoner of my natural body rhythms. So are you. So is everybody else. And these rhythms do not affect just our bodies, they affect our minds as well. We all have times when we think more effectively, and times when we should not be thinking at all.

THE RHYTHM OF DAY
AND NIGHT

Over the last two decades scientists have become increasingly aware of the existence and importance of bodily
cycles. Over every twenty-four-hour period our temperature,
blood pressure, red and white blood cell counts, hormonal
secretions, and an unknown number of other bodily functions alter in a regular rhythm. Practically every system of
the body has its own rhythm. The most dominant of these
rhythms are those that occur every twenty-four hours—the
circadian rhythms. But there are others that operate over
shorter periods, minutes and hours, or longer periods, weeks
and months.

All of these cycles interact with one another in ways that
scientists are just beginning to understand. But even at this
very early stage of exploring the cycles of the body and
mind you should learn to take advantage of your own
rhythms.

Scientists have assumed that the various physical cycles—
which can be measured—have an effect on mental states as
well. Studies with laboratory animals strongly indicate that
this is indeed the case. Laboratory animals appeared to remember training better when the training was given during
the first few hours of their normally active period than
during any other time of day.

Human mental activity is too complex, too subject to a
variety of outside influences, for me to make any flat statements about the best time of day for you to try to absorb new
material or to solve problems. There are, however, plenty of
studies to indicate that certain times of day regularly are
better for mental activity than others. Scores on memory

tests and problem-solving tests vary greatly for the same individual at different times of day. But just what times are best for you is very much of an individual matter. You will have to figure it out for yourself.

How? Simple. In Chapter 4 I suggested that if you wanted to know what really happened in your past you had to keep a diary. If you want to know what your mental state is during the course of a twenty-four-hour period, you have to keep a written record.

Here is a sample, my own written record for today.

8 A.M. Awake, but very sluggish.
9 A.M. Still sluggish, not really getting started.
10 A.M. Not thinking effectively—doing busywork.
11 A.M. Finally got to work, though slowly.

Between the hours of noon and four I had lunch and went out and did not keep track of my mental state.

4 P.M. Back at work and beginning to move along.
5 P.M. Still working effectively but beginning to get hungry.
6 P.M. Dinner.
7 P.M. Back at work, and for the first time today my mind feels really clear.
8 P.M. I am typing this segment at this moment. I still feel sharp and will probably continue to work until 10.

That is a fairly typical day for me. I don't really need to keep this sort of a record anymore. For many years I have been very interested in the subject of biological and mental cycles, and therefore have been acutely aware of my own.

How much do you know about yours? The first thing that you must do is simply be aware of the fact that these cycles do exist, and that they are extremely powerful controlling factors in your life. I am simply amazed at the number of people who deny that such rhythms exist—at least for them. They try to bull their way through a day as if every hour were just the same as every other hour. They think they can keep right on working until they drop. That's a bad way to live. You ignore the rhythms of your body at the risk of your physical and mental health.

So if you don't have a good idea of your own personal body and mind rhythms, keep a daily record—not just for a single day, but over a period of weeks, even months if possible. In a day or a week outside influences can distort the natural rhythms. Over an extended period of time these natural rhythms tend to reassert themselves—just as my evening working habits have always reasserted themselves, despite my persistent efforts to get on a more "normal" schedule.

INTERNAL AND EXTERNAL CLOCKS

Unfortunately, most of us live in a world in which our mental and physical activity is not governed by the internal rhythms, or internal clock, but by the clock on the wall. That is why so many of us try to ignore the internal clock altogether.

This is a fairly recent development in human history, and I don't think that we fully appreciate its significance yet. For most of human history our activities have had to conform to the natural rhythms of the earth—the rising and setting of the sun, the change of seasons, and so forth. The industrial revolution and such inventions as the electric light changed all of that. The factory system was not regulated by the rising and setting of the sun, or the change of seasons. It was ruled by the clock on the wall.

The pace of life has been greatly accelerated during the twentieth century and we have been removed further than

RE: THINKING

ever from nature. Many people spend their days working in buildings where they do not see the sun. All natural clues to the passage of time are obliterated, and we must rely entirely on a mechanical device, the clock. We work different and completely artificial schedules. When we travel we skip across time zones. Medical science is only now beginning to realize how destructive to health our persistent neglect of innate rhythms can be.

I'm not going to launch a plea for primitivism, or a paean to "the good old days" when we all lived on the land and got up with the sun. Such views are nostalgic nonsense, and ignore the harsh realities of starvation and disease, which were a regular feature of "the good old days." Nature is very cruel.

In any event, we cannot repeal the twentieth century. We must recognize the reality that much of our time is ruled by entirely artificial schedules. A student cannot go to his teacher and say, "Look here, sir, I'm really pretty slow at nine A.M. Why don't you reschedule my math test for eight in the evening? I'm sure I'll do much better." The student probably would do better, but I doubt if many teachers would consent to the request.

Nor would it do much good for you to go to your employer and say, "Two in the afternoon is a bad time for me mentally. What do you say we all get up early and have that important meeting at five in the morning? I'm really sharp then, and I'm sure I would be able to contribute much more."

That sort of rescheduling to fit our mental rhythms is obviously impractical. But there are some practical things that you can do.

USE YOUR MENTAL HIGHS

• There are bound to be certain hours in the regular nine-to-five day when your mind works better than at other times. If you have control over your work time, try to schedule important meetings and other periods in which decisions must be made to suit your mental highs—the times when you think best.

• If you hold an executive or supervisory position, try to find out about the mental rhythm of your subordinates. Notice whether Jones or Smith thinks better in the morning or afternoon. Don't be afraid to ask him what times are best for him. Keep in mind that these rhythms are innate. If someone does not seem to be giving full attention to his work at a particular time of day, it may simply mean that is his mental low point, not that he is goofing off. The more you can make work time coincide with mental highs, the better off everyone will be.

• Recognize that there are different kinds of mental activity, and different periods are better for each kind. Tests have shown that each of us has certain hours of the day when our minds are more receptive and we are able to learn better. Find out what your most mentally receptive times are by keeping a daily diary. This is particularly important if you are a student, or work at the sort of job in which you have to do a lot of reading of new material at home. Try to schedule your study sessions for your most receptive hours. You will find that you can absorb and remember more information in one good hour than three or four bad ones.

• Periods that are good for study do not necessarily coincide with periods that are best for doing problems or making decisions. Problem-solving ability usually peaks about an hour after the best time for learning ability. Find your own best time for this activity and use it. Students can do their math homework and business people can figure out the accounts during peak problem-solving times.

By making your mental activity coincide as much as possible with the daily peaks in your mental ability you can greatly increase your efficiency. You will not waste time dozing over your books, or making simple errors over and over again.

WHEN TO SHUT DOWN
YOUR MIND

It is just as important to know when not to think as it is to know when to think. Perhaps it is even more important.

F. Scott Fitzgerald wrote about three in the morning, when lost luggage seems like a death sentence. There are times of the day and night when we are at a physical and mental low and should not try to do any serious thinking. Indeed, there are times when it would be best not to think at all. For most people three in the morning is one of those times.

Thinking about important problems, and activities like trying to balance your checkbook, should not be undertaken before you go to bed. Insomnia is one of the nation's most widespread and persistent ailments, and it is a horror that is hard to explain to those who have never suffered from it. The reasons why some people have a lot of trouble sleeping are not fully known, but they are certainly mental as well as physical. Stimulating or upsetting mental activity just before bedtime tends to disrupt sleep, particularly in insomnia-prone people.

Besides, our energy level is usually very low just before

WHEN TO THINK (AND WHEN NOT TO)

going to bed. We are prone to gloomy thoughts, and we tend to give a negative cast to all our ideas.

Once again, keeping track of your daily mental ups and downs can be of great help. When you find those low periods you can say, "Look, I really don't want to think about that now. This is not a good time for me to make a decision." That's not procrastinating, it's simply recognizing the cycles of your body and mind and working in harmony with them.

Crossing time zones disrupts the physical and mental rhythms and results in the phenomenon known as "jet lag." Like seasickness, it has to be experienced to be believed. And as with seasickness, there are people who seem to be more prone to it than others. For years I didn't believe in it, because I had taken only short flights, across one or at most two time zones. When I took my first really long flight, it hit me. It was more than physical fatigue—I had expected that— it was a great deal of mental confusion as well. I was glad that I didn't have to make any important decisions within a day or two of getting off the plane.

Frequent travelers are aware of the dangers. In the opinion of Dr. C. C. Gullett, director of medical services for TWA, "People flying long distances should take this adjustment into account, especially diplomats, government leaders, military officials, businessmen and others who try to make important decisions after an extended flight."

The best advice about doing any hard thinking during a period when you are suffering from jet lag is, don't. Give yourself a day or so to adjust to the change in time zones.

Dr. Bertram Brown, former director of the National Institute of Mental Health, has said:

Not knowing that one has a time structure is like not knowing one has a heart or lungs. In every aspect of our physiology and lives, it becomes clear that we are made of the order we call time. As we look deeper into the

dimensions of our being, we may find that we too are
like the plant that flowers if given a little light at the
right time every seventy-two hours.

There may be in man a combination lock to his
activity and rest, his moods, illness and productiveness.
Moreover, by cultivation he may learn to utilize his subjective sense of time.

You certainly can—first by becoming aware of the fact
you have a time structure, and then by charting your own
daily, weekly, and monthly cycles.

SLEEP ON IT

Bits of folk wisdom are embodied in sayings like "Let me
sleep on the problem" and "It'll all look different in the
morning." These common beliefs are now backed up with
sound scientific evidence.

We have just been discussing the reasons why some
problems should not be confronted and some types of mental
activity not undertaken at certain times, particularly just
before your normal bedtime, when you are both physically
and mentally tired. When you wake up—presumably rested—
things do look different. You may be in far better shape to
confront and solve the problem.

But that's only part of it. The mind never completely
shuts off, even when we are asleep. There are dreams, of
course, but even when we are not dreaming our minds are
active. Just what goes on in our minds when we are asleep
remains largely unexplored territory for science, but there
is a wealth of anecdotal evidence to suggest that a certain
amount of unconscious problem solving actually does take
place while we are asleep.

There is a famous story about the German chemist

Friedrich Kekulé, who said that he solved the difficult problem of the atomic structure of the chemical benzene during
a dream. Kekulé was riding a bus when he dozed off and
began to dream. In the dream he saw atoms whirling in a
dance. Suddenly the tail end of one chain attached itself to
the head end "like a snake eating its tail." In Kekulé's dream
the atoms formed a spinning ring. And indeed, the atomic
structure of benzene is a ring.

Many writers have claimed that they got the idea for this
or that work during a dream, or the idea seemed to be fully
formed in their mind when they woke up in the morning.

That problems can be solved during sleep should not
really be surprising or mysterious. It fits well into the picture
of the process or stages of thought that has been developed
by many scholars and scientists of the past. Lists of the stages
differ slightly, but the basic idea behind them is the same.
Here are the stages listed in a book by James Webb Young
called *A Technique for Producing Ideas:*

1. The gathering of raw materials—both the materials of
your immediate problem and the materials that come from a
constant enrichment of your store of general knowledge.

2. The working over of these materials in your mind.

3. The incubating stage—when you let something besides
the conscious mind do the work of synthesis.

4. The actual birth of the idea—the "Eureka! I have it!"
stage.

5. The final shaping and developing of the idea to practical usefulness.

Webb's third stage, incubation, could easily take place
during sleep. The information and the previous mental work
that you have put in on a problem have not disappeared from
your mind. Even though you may not consciously be thinking about the problem—even though you are sound asleep—
your mind is still at work. With the conscious mind at rest,

the barriers to thought erected by old patterns and thinking habits are lowered. Your thoughts may flow in new ways and make unusual connections. Only after the new connections are made does the problem again rise to the conscious mind and—Eureka!—the problem has been solved.

That's why solutions to a problem so often come after a period of sleep, or at a time when you are not thinking about that particular problem. So the advice about sleeping on a problem is very good indeed.

It is also important to recognize that before any problem is solved there is very often a period of frustration—a time in which it seems that you are getting absolutely nowhere, that you are further from a solution than ever, and that it is all hopeless. The harder you think, the more hopeless it becomes.

The feeling is natural. Everybody experiences it from time to time. At moments like that you have to try to walk away from the problem for a while, take a nap if that is your habit, work in the garden, run around the block, jump up and down and scream. What you do doesn't make a lot of difference. One writer I know of has a pinball machine in his office. When he gets stuck he goes and plays pinball.

Relax, don't keep beating your head against it. Your mind is still at work on the problem, even when you are not consciously thinking about it. A solution is far more likely to emerge if you can get rid of your frustration by getting away from the problem for a while. It's like sleeping on it.

12

How to Give Your Mind a Break

BEATING MENTAL STRESS

Several times in this book I have pointed out that our minds are constantly being bombarded by stimuli and our brains are always at work. During sleep we dream, and even when we are not dreaming the brain is active, as half-formed thoughts and images flow through it. Problems are worked over and sometimes solved during sleep, and so it is often not as restful as we would like it to be.

During our waking hours our brains are always active, if not always very effective. During this period of history the human brain is under more stress than it ever was. We are exposed to more, and more vivid, stimuli (louder noises, brighter colors) than ever before. And it's getting worse. The average kid watches some twenty-five thousand TV commercials per year. We are also busier than ever before in history. When not actually working, we are doing something

RE: THINKING

else. Sports take mental as well as physical work; so (despite what many critics say) does watching television. Complete idleness—simply sitting doing nothing and thinking of nothing —is considered a sign of depression, even mental illness. How many hours a day do you just sit doing nothing? Do you consider that a desirable state? You probably think you are just "wasting time" and are itchy to "do something."

Yet "primitive" peoples spend a good deal of time sitting around thinking of nothing in particular. It's not laziness, it's just part of their way of life, and they see nothing wrong with it. Even the higher apes seem to spend a good deal of time in a state of apparent reverie. Periods of mental quiet— and techniques for inducing them—are a part of practically every religion, though they have been largely ignored and forgotten by modern Western religions.

The need for periods in which the mind can be switched off was largely denied in our busy modern cultures. In great numbers we turned to other relaxation devices, such as drugs and alcohol, which can be extremely harmful.

Then, during the early 1970s, this concept of mental quiet was introduced, or rather reintroduced, into Western society under the name of "meditation." The chief promoters of meditation were missionary gurus from India. At first it all seemed strange and exotic, and it attracted only the avant-garde, particularly in California. Then scientists began to test some of the claims that were made by the gurus, and lo and behold, it was discovered many of them were true! A variety of studies found that, properly done, meditation could produce a state of relaxation more profound than sleep.

When news of scientific confirmation of some of the meditation claims became widely known, the practice suddenly no longer seemed strange and exotic. Thousands, perhaps millions of perfectly ordinary people who would normally have nothing to do with Eastern religions plunged into meditation. It became a major nationwide fad.

But we Americans are chronic overdoers. Lots of people began to believe the more extreme claims made for meditation. Some supporters said it would make everybody happy, cure all sorts of stress-related diseases, even bring about world peace. Then the representatives of the most popular form of meditation began to claim that they could levitate—fly. That did it! Disappointed by meditation's failure to live up to all its extravagant claims, people turned away from it as quickly as they had once turned to it. A minority stuck to the practice, but by and large the great popular interest in meditation has disappeared and the traditional Western distrust of idleness has reasserted itself. And that's a real shame.

What is the subject of meditation doing in a book on thinking? That question is answered very neatly by the Indian writer Aubrey Menen in his book *The Mystics*. Menen complained there was a lot of "fudge" surrounding the subject: "The fudge is a pity, but it probably cannot be helped. The honest sort of Indian mystic has something very simple to say. He knows a way of putting our minds to rest without resorting to drink, or drugs, or a crack over the head with a hammer. It is a way of stopping your thinking. It has no appeal to people whose worry is that they never seem to have started: but more intelligent people do often feel that they need a holiday from their own minds, while leaving them intact to come home to when the holiday is over." When properly used, meditation really works, and it's easy to do. By giving your mind a rest you will be able to think more effectively.

WHAT MEDITATION CAN
AND CAN'T DO

For those of you who have never meditated, I'll tell you how. For those of you who have drifted away from the practice, this should serve as a timely reminder.

Before turning to the practical instructions on how to use this technique to lower mental stress, I had better make clear just exactly what the aim is.

If you are looking for a religious experience, enlightenment, total bliss, a cure for all that ails you, or a way to levitate, look elsewhere. I offer no judgments as to the validity of any of these claims (except the one about levitation, which is utterly fraudulent). There are plenty of books around that will give you instructions in reaching these goals.

The aim of this chapter is limited, simple, and very practical. I'm going to provide you with a method of reducing mental stress by giving your mind a rest. This method will help you break the worry cycle, which all of us become caught up in from time to time. It will help you free your mind for constructive thought. If other benefits flow from the use of this technique, well and good, but there will be no grand promises. That's what killed the meditation boom in the first place.

There are many meditation techniques that can be used. The one that I recommend is the one developed by Dr. Herbert Benson of Boston's Beth Israel Hospital and explained in his book *The Relaxation Response*. I like it because the language in which it is described is simple and unmystical, and therefore conforms more closely with the way we act and think in the West in the twentieth century. It isn't necessarily superior just because it happens to be Western and was developed by a scientist. It is nearly identical to other meditation systems, but the Benson method just seems to be more congenial to this time and place than some of the Eastern or religiously oriented techniques.

THE FOUR BASIC ELEMENTS

Investigators have found that no matter what the meditative technique, and no matter what culture it came from, all shared four basic elements.

1. *A quiet environment.* In order to meditate the person must choose a calm and quiet place. Since historically meditation has usually been associated with religion, much of it has been done in the quiet of a church, temple, or monastery, but the religious nature of the setting was not the essential part. The quiet was.

2. *A mental device.* All techniques involved some constant stimulus upon which attention could be fixed. The popular meditative techniques of the 1970s used a mantra— a simple word that was silently repeated over and over again to fix attention. A good deal of confusion was centered around the mantra. It came to be looked upon as some sort of secret, magic word. In fact, any simple word will do, for it is only a device. Some meditative techniques involve gazing at an object, often a religious object such as a cross or holy picture, but repeating the mantra seems easier for beginners. The mental device keeps the meditator's mind from wandering by breaking a train of thought and bringing it back to the device. Hindu meditators used a Sanskrit word. Christian meditators have used a word like *love* or *God*.

3. *A passive attitude.* This is the hardest part of it, for we are not by nature a passive people. Meditators are told to ignore distracting thoughts and not worry about them.

RE: THINKING

They are also taught not to worry about how they are doing, but just adopt a "let it happen" attitude and return to concentration on their mental device. Writes Benson, "The passive attitude is perhaps the most important element in eliciting the Relaxation Response."

4. *A comfortable position.* Some meditators believed that you had to adopt the cross-legged lotus position or some other unnatural and exotic posture. Not true; you simply need to be comfortable. But you can't get too comfortable or you may fall asleep, and that is not what you are supposed to do. The lotus position and some of the other relatively difficult postures assumed by meditators may have evolved to keep them from falling asleep.

HOW TO DO IT

Now that the four basic elements have been identified, here is how Benson and his associates suggest that you can apply them in your daily life. The Benson system is really just another adaptation of the popular Transcendental Meditation system, which is itself basically an adaptation of earlier Indian techniques.

1. Find a quiet place where you are not likely to be disturbed for twenty minutes or so. Absolute quiet is not essential; many people who took up meditation found that they could do it while they were commuting on a train. Since most forms of meditation are done with the eyes closed, fellow passengers thought they were asleep. Others, who had some difficulty finding a nondistracting environment, would pop into a church, not to pray but to find a quiet place to meditate.

2. Sit down in a comfortable position and close your eyes.

HOW TO GIVE YOUR MIND A BREAK

3. Relax, or at least relax as much as you are able to. Try the technique of first relaxing the muscles of your feet and then moving upward. Complete relaxation is not necessary, because you are not trying to go to sleep.

4. Breathe through your nose, easily and naturally. Every time you breathe out silently repeat the word "one." That is to be your mental device, your mantra. Breathe in, breathe out "one." Breathe in, breathe out "one."

5. Do this for ten to twenty minutes, twice a day if possible. You can open your eyes to check on the time, but don't worry too much about it. Don't set an alarm of any sort—that will just provoke anxiety as you wait for it to go off. After the meditation period is finished continue to sit quietly for a few minutes without meditating. It is suggested that at first you sit with your eyes closed, but as you become more practiced you can sit with your eyes open.

6. While you are sitting and repeating "one" don't worry about achieving anything. Don't worry if you begin to feel fidgety, or if you do not reach a state of deep relaxation. You are not trying to go anywhere. Just let it happen. If distracting thoughts occur, simply try to ignore them and go back to repeating "one." For a while you may feel that you are getting nowhere, that you are not relaxing at all. Don't be concerned. With practice you get better at this technique and you will automatically relax.

There are two notes of caution. First, you are advised not to try the Benson system, or any other meditative technique, for two hours after eating. For some unknown reason, the digestive process seems to interfere with the technique.

Second, there are a small number of people who are in a state of extremely high anxiety and tension, for whom the process does not work, and indeed may make things worse. For such individuals, sitting quietly opens the mind to more anxiety-provoking thoughts, and a simple mental device like silently repeating "one" is not enough to break the train of disturbing thoughts. If you try the technique and find your self becoming more rather than less anxious, it simply may not be for you, so give it up.

People who are undergoing psychotherapy also have some difficulty with meditation. Meditation teaches you to discard thoughts, and not to follow a line of thought. In psychotherapy patients are often encouraged to free-associate and to follow a train of thought where it leads. The two techniques seem to be contradictory, so the patient in therapy may not benefit from any form of meditation, at least during a period of active treatment.

Needless to say, using drugs or alcohol during meditation is strictly discouraged. The technique is supposed to be an entirely natural way of relaxing.

BREAKING THE WORRY CYCLE

Those who find a meditative technique impossible to use or are actually harmed by it are very much in the minority. If you are among the great majority, the technique can help you. At the very least it will give you a chance twice a day to break out of destructive thought patterns.

Thinking is considered a virtue, but the mere process of thought is not a virtue in and of itself. Thinking must have a point; if it doesn't, it can be useless or worse. One problem that most of us face is that sometimes we think too much, or at least at inappropriate times, and in pointless and circular ways that are destructive.

When we turn a bothersome problem over and over in our mind at night, we rarely arrive at a worthwhile solution.

HOW TO GIVE YOUR MIND A BREAK

Generally all that happens is that we lose sleep and become anxious and depressed. Thinking becomes worry—basically they are the same thing; it's just that one will help you and the other will not. Some people try to make a virtue out of an affliction by arguing that "only intelligent people worry." This is simply not true. Worry is the enemy of productive thinking.

Take Charles, for example, a bright fellow, but a big worrier. One morning when he got up for work he found that his car wouldn't start. He had to hustle to catch a bus. All the way in he worried about being late for work, and when he finally got there he began to worry about his car. What was wrong with it? Could he get it fixed in time for work tomorrow? Would the repairs be expensive? Would he be forced to buy a new car? Could he afford such an expense? And so on and so on.

He thought, or worried, about the problem from every possible angle. Of course, there was absolutely nothing he could do at the moment. The result was that he wasted an entire day in pointless and draining mental activity. During the course of that day he confronted a number of problems that would have benefited from constructive thought, but his mind was occupied elsewhere. I'm quite sure most of you recognize the pattern.

Dr. Benson's Relaxation Response or any other simple meditative technique will help to break the cycle of worry. If Charles could take twenty minutes out of his afternoon to sit quietly, relax, and think of nothing but his breathing and the silent repetition of the word "one," he wouldn't have to lose an entire day to pointless worry. Over a period of time the repeated use of such a technique would tend to lower his general level of anxiety, and so such destructive and circular patterns of thought would be less likely to start up in the first place. The success of meditation does not depend on your willpower. Relaxation is a natural and for most people inevitable biological response to the technique.

YOU WON'T BE BRAINWASHED

During the period when meditation became a fad, along with the excessive claims made for the practice, there were also excessive fears expressed.

Some of the fears were based simply on religious prejudice, though this was not often acknowledged. The meditative practices that became most common were based on systems used in India by Hindus, so there was a suspicion that meditation was an exotic form of Hinduism, that it would somehow draw the unsuspecting away from their traditional religions. The fact that nearly identical forms of meditation were once common Christian practices was not acknowledged, or even known. Nor were people who feared the pratice much reassured that it could be carried out effectively in an entirely nonreligious context. It still seemed strange, exotic, and evil.

Another fear was that adopting a passive attitude for two short periods every day would somehow lead to a general personality change, that would make one more passive in general. Most of this fear was based on simple misunderstanding. (A bit of subtle prejudice may have been operating here as well, in linking the "Oriental" practice with a view of the "passive Oriental," as opposed to the "active Westerner.")

It is possible that *excessive* meditation—meditation for hours every day—may produce a profound behavioral change over a long period of time. But there is no evidence at all that the brief periods of meditation recommended here have any negative effects. Far from becoming passive, an in-

HOW TO GIVE YOUR MIND A BREAK

dividual who is able to free himself from destructive patterns of anxiety and worry will have more energy and be more active.

If you are able to give your mind a rest, you will become a better thinker.

13

Thinking with Both Sides of Your Brain

WHAT KIND OF THINKER ARE YOU?

Try this little quiz.

1. I consider myself:
   A. artistic
   B. logical
2. When confronted with a problem I try to:
   A. wait for an inspiration
   B. work it through
3. In card games I prefer
   A. poker
   B. bridge
4. I feel more comfortable
   A. at a dance
   B. at a cocktail party

5. Which of the following statements do I consider
   most accurate?
   A. If you have to explain it you ain't got it.
   B. The unexamined life is not worth living.
6. Which of the following statements applies to me?
   A. I feel discussions and arguments are a waste of
      time.
   B. I enjoy discussions and arguments.
7. How do I rate myself?
   A. I have a lot of good ideas but have difficulty
      carrying them through.
   B. I am a person who develops plans carefully.
8. I often feel:
   A. that the people around me rarely use their minds
      effectively
   B. that people talk too much without any result
9. I agree most closely with the following statement:
   A. I like to get the "big picture."
   B. Attention to detail is the key to success.
10. When I meet a new person I:
    A. tend to rely on my instincts as to whether to trust
       him or not
    B. reserve judgment and try to find out more about
       him.

If you picked answer A for eight or more of these questions you probably rely heavily on the right half of your
brain. If you picked B you are more likely a left-brain
thinker.

Right brain? Left brain? Don't we just have one brain?
No, we don't, and the recognition of this fundamental fact
represents one of the most significant advances in understanding how we think of the last several centuries.

TWO KINDS OF THINKING

We have always sort of recognized that there are two kinds of thinking, and these two different modes of thought are usually set in opposition to each other: reason versus inspiration; conscious versus unconscious; logic versus feeling; head versus heart.

Though the power of "inspiration" and "feeling" to influence our thinking and behavior have long been acknowledged, they have not really been considered part of "proper thinking." Indeed, they were generally considered to be opposed to "proper thinking," and those who wanted to "think clearly" were advised to avoid allowing them to influence the mental processes.

For several hundred years most people, in the West at least, assumed that the only proper way to think was in an orderly, step-by-step, rational manner. That's the sort of thinking that we have been discussing throughout much of this book. But it is really only half of the thinking story. Step-by-step thinking can not adequately explain the moments of intuition and inspiration that we all have experienced from time to time. These moments are something beyond the conscious working through at problems that we discussed previously.

Sometimes these nonrational experiences have resulted in profound insights, or even caused us to change our way of life. Yet because such experiences were impossible to describe adequately they were often overlooked, or brushed aside as unimportant by scientists. They were not "thinking" and thus deserved no serious consideration.

That has changed, for science now has a pretty good

idea where these flashes of intuition and inspiration come from, and a new appreciation of their importance in our lives. They are indeed "thinking," but they come from a part of our brain that we have long ignored.

In fact, it isn't even proper to talk about "our brain," for in reality we have two brains, not one. They are a left brain and a right brain, and they can operate in startlingly different ways. If we are to take full advantage of that most marvelous of organs, our brain, we must first understand how these two brains function and how to appreciate and use the products of both halves.

TWO KINDS OF BRAIN

If you have ever looked at a model or diagram of the human brain you noticed that the brain is divided into two apparently identical halves, the right hemisphere and the left hemisphere. These halves are connected by a thick bundle of nerves called the corpus callosum.

For a while it was assumed that since the two halves of the brain looked alike they simply duplicated each other's functions. But many physicians realized that this wasn't absolutely true. People who received injuries to the left side of their brain often lost muscular functions on the right side of the bodies, and vice versa. A stroke that damaged the left hemisphere might cause paralysis of the right arm. For some reason the muscular controls of the brain are crossed.

But as far as the mental functions of the brain were concerned, it was still assumed that they were diffused generally and equally through both halves of the brain. Yet there was some clinical evidence to dispute that assumption, too. For example, people who had received injuries to the left side of their brain sometimes lost the power of speech. People who received injuries to the right side of their brain almost never did. Gradually scientists realized that certain strictly mental functions, most notably speech, were centered in the left side of the brain.

Were there any special mental functions centered in the physically identical right side of the brain? At first it didn't seem so. But that imbalance looked suspicious. A long series of different experiments by scientists all over the world finally showed that the right side of the brain had its own special mental functions. The reason the right-brain functions were so hard to identify is that all the verbal skills were on the other side. The right brain couldn't "talk about" itself, so it was ignored.

DOES THE RIGHT HAND KNOW
WHAT THE LEFT IS DOING?

In the 1960s Dr. Roger Sperry of the California Institute of Technology was studying a very interesting patient. He called the man W.J. W.J. was an ex-soldier who had received severe head injuries during the war; as a result, he began to suffer from seizures, which became worse and worse. In desperation, surgeons finally severed his corpus callosum. After the operation W.J. felt much better, the seizures disappeared, and he appeared normal. But he wasn't. W.J. had become truly a man with a "split personality."

Remember the old saying about the left hand not knowing what the right hand is doing? That was literally true of W.J. His left hand, controlled by the right half of his brain, not only did not know what his right hand was doing, it couldn't understand instructions. All the verbal faculties are located in the left half of the brain. To make matters stranger still, W.J.'s right brain seemed aggressive and unreliable. At one point W.J. attempted to strike his wife with his left hand, while his right hand tried to stop it.

One of Sperry's graduate students, Michael Gazzaniga, visited W.J. one day. The two were playing horseshoes in the back yard when the student saw W.J. pick up an ax with his antisocial left hand. At this point he decided to leave in a hurry. Gazzaniga later said, "It was entirely likely that the more aggressive right hemisphere might be in control." Gazzaniga knew that he couldn't reason with the right hemisphere because it didn't understand language. He feared that he might become part of a test case: "Which half-brain does society punish or execute?"

W.J.'s case is obviously—and fortunately—a rare one. In normal brains where the corpus callosum is intact, information flows freely between the two brain halves. The left hand does know what the right is doing. But there are still vast differences between the functions of the two halves. The differences, however, are not inborn; they develop as a human being grows. Young children who have had serious brain injuries are able to compensate for them far more easily than an adult can. If a child under the age of five or even ten has a massive injury to the left half of his brain, he will still be able to learn to speak, though with difficulty. If there is an injury to the right half of the brain the child will experience about the same degree of speaking difficulty. Language has not yet been firmly fixed in one hemisphere of the brain. An adult who loses speech due to a left-brain injury will not be able to learn to speak again, but speech is unaffected if the injury is confined to the right brain.

COMPETITION IN THE BRAIN

As the brain develops and different mental functions come to be located in one or the other hemisphere, the two hemispheres appear to compete with each other for dominance. Says Dr. Sperry, "excellence in one tends to interfere with top-level performance in the other." Thus, one side of the brain inevitably comes to dominate the other. Western societies are built on language and on rational step-by-step thinking, which requires language. These are the mental processes centered in the left brain. For most of us the left brain is the dominant one. But we ignore the function of the nonverbal, nonrational right half of our brain at our peril. To think properly, we must make use of the talents of both halves.

And this brings us to Robert Ornstein, a California psychologist who has done more than anyone else to awaken the public to left-brain and right-brain activity.

Like so many ideas about the brain, the idea that it contains two different forms of thought, essentially two different kinds of consciousness, is not really new, as Ornstein points out in an article in *Psychology Today:* "The belief there are two forms of consciousness has been with us for centuries. Reason versus passion is one of its guises, mind versus intuition another. The feminine, the sacred, the mysterious historically have lined up against the masculine, the profane and the logical. Medicine argues with art, yin complements yang. In fable and folklore, religion and science, this dualism has recurred with stunning regularity."

But now science was now able to locate the places where these two different forms of consciousness originated. It could now be shown that they had a definite physiological base and were not just the result of differences in culture or philosophy, or simply illusions. One form of consciousness originated in the left side of the brain, the other in the right.

The electroencephalograph is a sensitive machine that measures the electrical activity of the brain. It has been one of the most useful tools in unlocking the mysteries of the brain. Most researchers assume that thoughts are transmitted at least in part by electrical impulses. Thus, when the brain is working—that is, thinking—electrical activity increases. The electroencephalograph is sensitive enough not only to measure electrical activity of the brain as a whole, but to pinpoint where in the brain the electrical activity is at its greatest.

Ornstein and his colleagues have tested large numbers of people with the electroencephalograph and have found that during certain tasks the left side of the brain is most active, while during others it is the right side of the brain that generates more electrical impulses.

Subjects who were asked to arrange colored blocks and designs showed increased right-brain activity, while their left hemisphere remained relatively quiet. When the same subjects were switched to a verbal activity like letter writing, the activity of the brain picked up on the left side and died down on the right. The same pattern was observed when the subjects were asked just to think about writing a letter.

Other activities that stimulated the left brain were reading a column of print, doing arithmetic, and making up a list of words beginning with a particular letter. When the subjects were asked to remember a musical tone or draw a simple design, the right brain took over again.

Under ideal circumstances the two halves of the brain should cooperate with each other, each taking up the task for which it is best suited. In reality, Ornstein believes, the two halves of the brain are not in perfect balance and one half tends to dominate the other. "Most people are dominated by one mode or the other," he says. "They either have difficulty in dealing with crafts and body movements, or difficulty with language."

LIMITATIONS OF BOOK LEARNING

In some circles it is popular to knock "book learning" as something impractical and inferior to practical experience. Generally such criticisms are a defense by people who lack education and are embarrassed by this. But there really are things that you can't learn from books or lectures or any other verbal source. These are activities controlled by the right brain.

I have always been fascinated by magic. I once tried to work up a little magic act for my own amusement. I bought a batch of magic tricks with instructions and started to practice. I was hopeless. Though I knew how the tricks were done, I could never pull them off properly. My few performances before my family were greeted with groans and hoots.

"You've got the other card in your hand, I can see it" was a typical comment.

Finally I gave up in disgust and despair.

Later I discussed this dismal experience with my magician friend, the creator of the "mechanical hands" (Chapter 2). "You made a common mistake," he told me. "You thought you could learn magic from an instruction sheet. Most people just can't do it, not very well anyway. You have to have someone show you how to do it, and guide you through it step by step. You have to develop a feel for the trick. Magic is a performance. It's not what you do, but how you do it. Most tricks are basically simple. Anybody can learn how they are done, but that doesn't mean they can do them properly."

He then proceeded to demonstrate by showing me a couple of the tricks that I had tried so unsuccessfully to perform. Though I knew how the tricks were done and I watched him closely, I still couldn't see how he did them— that's magic.

Have you ever met anyone who learned to ski or play tennis or ride a bike by reading about how to do it, or by verbal instruction alone? You can learn difficult math or subtle forms of philosophy from books, but not the simple act of roller skating. Someone has to show you how, and you have to practice. The left brain may understand the instructions perfectly, but it is the right brain that controls the activity, and the words don't mean anything to the right brain. Learning simple physical activities does not start in the muscles. It starts in the nonverbal right hemisphere of the brain.

While the two modes of thought can complement each other, they do not readily replace each other. To test this, Ornstein suggests, try to describe a spiral staircase without using your hands. You can't do it; words are not enough.

CAN YOU WALK AND CHEW GUM AT THE SAME TIME?

Lyndon Johnson was once reported to have quipped that Gerald Ford could not walk and chew gum at the same time. The comment was, of course, an insult, implying that Ford was so stupid that he couldn't carry on two simple activities at once. But the comment also, probably accidentally, touched upon a profound truth about the way our double brain operates. It *is* hard to perform certain activities at the same time. Walking and chewing gum are not included, for gum chewing is virtually an automatic act, but there are other physical activities that are not automatic and do involve considerable brain activity.

Marcel Kinsbourne of Duke University devised a simple test of the conflict that can develop between the right and the left brains. Ask a friend to balance an ordinary wooden dowel first on the index finger of the right hand, then on the index finger of the left hand. It's not a particularly difficult task, although usually right-handed people do better with the right hand while left-handed people do better with the left.

Now ask your friend to speak while balancing the dowel, and measure the time that he is able to keep the dowel balanced. Kinsbourne found that the balancing time of right-handed people using their right hand fell off sharply. Talking (a left-brain activity) placed an extra burden on the left brain. But remember that muscular control is crossed, so balancing with the right hand is also controlled by the left brain. The left hand, which is controlled by the right brain, either was unaffected, or balancing time actually increased. The right brain has nothing to do with talking.

Ask a friend how to spell a long word like *Minnesota*, then look into his eyes. In most cases his eyes will shift to the right, indicating that the left part of the brain has been activated.

Not all questions will produce a rightward shift of the eyes. Ornstein believes that the kind of question you ask will affect the way the eyes shift, because different kinds of questions activate different halves of the brain. Spelling *Minnesota* is a verbal question, so the left brain is brought into play.

Such activities as spatial relations are centered in the right brain. So ask someone, "Which way does George Washington face on a quarter?" That is a spatial question. In most cases eyes will shift to the left, for the right hemisphere controls our ability to deal with spatial relations.

Electroencephalograph tests by Ornstein and others have demonstrated that the type of job you have is closely related to which side of your brain is dominant. In one test a group of lawyers, people in a profession that employs verbal and reasoning skills, were tested against a like number of sculptors and ceramic artists, professions in which spatial relations are more important. The lawyers were shown to have more active left brains, while the sculptors and ceramic artists had more active right brains. But are some of us born lawyers and others born sculptors? Not necessarily.

GOOD MIND OR GOOD MOUTH

While the type of brain we have, whether the left or right hemisphere is dominant, may in large measure determine what sort of career we pursue, it is probable that most of us are born with an equal chance to be either left- or right-brained. The dominance of one half of the brain over the other is cultural rather than hereditary. Western society tends to put more stress on the rational and verbal—that is, the left-brain activities. Therefore, most of us tend to regard only left-brain activities as signs of intelligence. The more left-brained someone is, the more intelligent he is supposed to be. As a result, we often say that someone has a good mind when in reality all he has is a good mouth.

The failure to understand that there are two different kinds of mental activity can be destructive. Intellectuals have often scorned as "stupid" the visual artist and the athlete who could not use words well. Artists and athletes respond with equal scorn, regarding the talky intellectual as out of touch with what is real and important. In many schools there is a wide split between the eggheads and the jocks. The brains of both groups simply operate in different ways, without one being necessarily superior to the other.

Children growing up in most white middle-class families in America tend to grow up in a left-brain-environment. Words and step-by-step thinking are not only valued, they are viewed as the key to future success in most professions.

But in some parts of our society the right hemisphere predominates. Children in poor black neighborhoods, for example, learn to use the right hemisphere. Under such conditions they grow up being better at sports and music, poorer at verbal tasks. The left-brain person has trouble with physical movements, because his left hemisphere tends to analyze the movements, and that slows him down.

There is a hilarious sequence in the film *Silver Streak* that demonstrates this. Disguised as a black, Gene Wilder is trying to escape from a train station. His tutor in this deception is black comedian Richard Pryor. Wilder puts on blackface, changes his clothes, holds a portable radio to his ear, and tries to walk "cool," but he just can't do it. No matter how many times Pryor corrects him, he still can't get the walk right. Finally Pryor decides that the deception is good enough to get him past the white guards, but "You better hope we don't meet any Black Muslims."

EXPLAINING THE UNEXPLAINABLE

While conventional wisdom in the West has held that if you can't explain it, it's somehow not important, religions, and particularly Eastern religions, have always had quite a different attitude. These religions appreciated the power and often the essential "rightness" of inspiration. Since inspiration is nonverbal, they have tried to convey its power and wisdom in a variety of stories and parables that our left-brain culture has a lot of trouble understanding. Robert Ornstein is very fond of quoting from the teaching tales of the Sufis, a mystical sect of Islam. Teaching tales are short, simple stories told to make a point, much like the parables of the Bible. These tales, says Ornstein, have a lot to tell us about how we think, and how we should think. Here is a little tale told about a Sufi saint named Mojud:

Early in his life Mojud was a nobody, an undistinguished inspector of weights and measures in a small town. There was nothing about his personality or previous life that would make him appear a candidate for sainthood. Then one day "Khidr, the mysterious guide of the Sufis, appeared to him, dressed in shimmering green."

Khidr instructed Mojud to give up his job, go down to the river, take off his clothes, and jump in. "Perhaps someone will save you."

Since Sufis are not allowed to speak directly of Khidr, Mojud could not explain his actions. His friends simply assumed that he had gone mad.

Mojud jumped in the river, but he could not swim. The current carried him downstream, where he was picked up by some fishermen. They also thought he was mad, but, being friendly people, they took him in anyway, and he worked for a while as a fisherman.

After that Mojud wandered about, stopping to work in one place, then another. He always left on mysterious and thoroughly inexplicable instructions from Khidr. After some years people ceased to regard Mojud as a madman, and began thinking of him as something of a saint. He got the reputation of being able to heal the sick and perform other miracles.

But when people asked him how he had come to his saintly position, he was unable to explain. "So," says the storyteller, "the biographers constructed for Mojud a wonderful and exciting history; because all saints must have their story, and their story must be in accordance with the appetite of the listener, not the realities of life."

This is not a story of a petty bureaucrat who suddenly began doing crazy things on the instructions of a green-robed spirit and wound up a saint. It is a story that shows that people can be impelled to do strange and inexplicable things that are good, and even saintly, and that these actions should be respected even if they are not understood.

Most of us raised in Western culture hold fast to the belief that we should always be able to explain our motives and discuss our thoughts. Anything beyond explanation is considered the product of an inferior kind of thinking, perhaps of not thinking at all. We would simply consider Mojud a madman. The Sufis, says Robert Ornstein, know better—they grasp the fact that there are other ways to think, and that these ways cannot be explained in a manner that is familiar to us. That's why they use teaching tales.

The Sufis are not the only ones to hold that there is more than one way of thinking. There is, for example, the story of the famous Hasidic rabbi who was to visit the Jewish community of a small Russian town. This visit was a great event and the men of the town spent many hours preparing questions to ask the celebrated wise man. All the men gathered in the largest room in the town for the rabbi's visit.

But when the rabbi finally arrived he said nothing. He just sat silently in front of the anxious group for a few moments. Then he began to softly hum a Hasidic tune. Soon the others in the room began to hum along with him. Then he began to sing. Soon everyone was singing. Then he began to sway back and forth, and finally to dance, and soon everyone in the room was caught up in the dance.

At first the dancing was restrained and self-conscious,

but as it continued the men became more and more deeply involved in it. Dancing engaged the whole of their attention. After the dancing had gone on for a while, the rabbi gradually slowed down and stopped. He looked at the group and said, "I trust I have answered all of your questions." Then he left.

Just as the Sufi tale is not really about a spirit in a green outfit, this Hasidic story is not about dancing. It is about thinking. The rabbi knew, from long experience, that by dancing the men would be inspired and find their own answers to the questions that had been troubling them.

The Sufis and the Hasidim are mystical sects. The mystic does not try to think about things rationally, and flashes of inspiration are both expected and encouraged. However, there are plenty of nonmystics who have reported very similar experiences.

The poet Amy Lowell, in a discussion of how she composed her poems, said, "A common phrase among poets is, 'it just came to me.' So hackneyed has this become that one learns to suppress the expression with care, but really it is the best description I know of the conscious arrival of a poem."

"That's fine for mystics and poets," you say, "but their minds don't work the same way as the rest of our minds do. After all, didn't Shakespeare, the greatest of poets, say: 'The lunatic, the lover and the poet/ Are of imagination all compact'?"

But haven't you had mental experiences that in many ways parallel those reported by the mystic and the poet? Perhaps there has been a problem that has been bothering you for months. Then one day, quite suddenly the solution is there in your head, and from the moment it comes to you you know with complete confidence that the solution is the correct one. Maybe you had agonized over making a decision.

You had gone over all the possible angles in your mind a hundred times. Then in an instant, and for no obvious reason, the decision is made and you have no more doubts. You can't really explain why you made the decision—because it was made in the right half of your brain.

INTUITION, FEMININE AND MASCULINE

Even though we may not like to admit it, many of the important decisions we make in our lives are based on "illogical" right-brain activity. We get the idea, and make up the reasons for it afterward. Society in general once assigned this sort of intuitive thinking only to women—"feminine intuition," it was called. The term was one of condescension, almost a joke. Feminine intuition was an inferior form of mental activity, because women were not supposed to think very well. While the accuracy of "feminine intuition" was sometimes grudgingly admitted, it was never taken seriously.

Of course, men also relied on their intuition, though they just didn't admit it, even to themselves. Men had "hunches" or "insights," and even these were not generally acknowledged. Most men were able to successfully rationalize their actions with a host of after-the-fact reasons, which had nothing to do with the original decision but sounded good.

Take the case of Diana. In a less liberated era she might have referred to her "woman's intuition." She is known for having an uncanny knack of being able to judge a person's character, even know what they are thinking. Her friends have jokingly referred to her as being psychic. When she was little, schoolmates called her a witch. Diana adamantly denies possessing any "supernatural" abilities; she doesn't be-

THINKING WITH BOTH SIDES OF YOUR BRAIN

lieve in them. She says anybody can do what she does if they "trust their feelings, and don't let their prejudices get in the way."

Diana's friend Janet was just coming out of an emotionally shattering divorce. One night at a party she met Steve, who was also recently divorced. They seemed to hit it off immediately, and were rapidly involved in a passionate affair. Janet told herself that Steve was everything she had always hoped for in a man, and he appeared to be dead serious about her. Janet desperately wanted to make an emotional commitment, but she was afraid and held back. There was something about Steve that made her slightly uncomfortable. She rationalized that she was being overcautious because she had been burned before.

Steve pressed her. He wanted her to go with him to California, where he had just gotten a new job. Finally the anguished Janet called Diana to talk about her dilemma.

"Steve says he loves me, but how can I be sure? I'll be giving up a lot if I leave. But if I don't I may lose him forever. What should I do?"

It was a bad moment for Diana. The first time she had met Steve, she felt an instant stab of distrust. The feeling had not abated during subsequent meetings, and she had come to genuinely dislike the fellow. She had never said anything to Janet, because she felt it was not her business to do so, and because she could offer no concrete reasons for her opinions. Now she was being put on the spot. It was worse because Janet didn't really want advice. She had already decided she was going with Steve. All she wanted was confirmation of her decision.

Should Diana try to prevent her friend from making what she was convinced was a serious mistake, by telling her the truth as she saw it? Or should she try to sidestep the whole question? Diana knew that would be the equivalent of telling Janet to go to California with Steve.

Diana opted to tactfully, gently, but firmly tell the truth. She got no thanks for it. Janet was furious. She shouted that Diana was "prejudiced" against Steve, and that she was "jealous of the happiness Steve and I have found." She angrily hung up the phone. And she went ahead and did what she had already decided to do anyway, go off to California with Steve.

Eight months later she was back. Steve had been a disaster. Once they got to California Steve seemed to change. He revealed himself as being selfish, callous, almost brutal. Janet had made a deep emotional commitment and didn't want to let go, but ultimately Steve found another (and much younger) woman and threw Janet out of the apartment they shared (for which Janet had put up most of the money).

Janet apologized to Diana for the way she had acted, and was deeply sorry not to have listened to her in the first place. Yet Diana's insights into Steve's character were not so astonishing. Even Janet had "felt" there was something wrong with him. She simply refused to listen to her feelings.

A GOOD EYE, GOOD EAR, GOOD MIND

People who are predominantly left-brain types sometime have trouble seeing "the whole picture." They get hung up on details. My wife and I have both run into this problem when trying to decorate a house. We are both perfectly capable of picking out a nice piece of furniture, attractive wallpaper or curtains. But all of these items are viewed individually, without any ability to visualize what the total effect might be. On a couple of occasions I have been unpleasantly surprised at the total effect produced by my efforts at interior decoration. It's not that I don't try, or don't know what I want. It's just that I lack the ability to visualize the complete picture.

In most cases we call in an artist friend who is quite different. She can walk into a room armed only with a swatch of wallpaper or a paint sample and almost instantly get a total picture of what the room will look like. She has, we have often remarked, a "good eye."

We also speak of musicians as having a "good ear," and when we see an athlete like Dr. J make one of his impossible shots we are apt to remark that he has "great reflexes." But these activities—the "eye," the "ear," and the "reflexes"—are all controlled by the brain, just as surely as are the activities of the successful lawyer or mathematician. It's just a different part of the brain that is in control. It is a measure of the prejudices of our society that only those who excel in left-brain activities are described as having a "good mind."

WHEN THE RIGHT BRAIN
TAKES OVER

Because we cannot "talk" to the right brain and words cannot be used to describe its activities, it remains by far the more mysterious part of our consciousness. The left brain appears to process information in the logical step-by-step manner that we normally call thinking. The right brain also processes information, but in an entirely different way. It seems to handle information from all sorts of sources all at once. While the left brain takes in a bit at a time, the right brain gets the whole picture.

For most of us, most of the time, the left brain is in

control. But sometimes, suddenly and without warning, the right brain briefly takes over. In the laboratory scientists have occasionally been surprised by an unexpected surge in electrical activity from the right hemisphere of a subject's brain. Briefly the normally subordinate right half takes over. It is this sudden dominance of the right brain that may account for those sudden flashes of inspiration. Though we do not yet know how or why this comes about, it is quite apparent that there is nothing mystical or illusionary about what we call inspiration. And it is *not* just step-by-step thinking carried on unconsciously.

Thus, while step-by-step thinking is fine most of the time, inspiration—a message from the other side of our brain—is a real phenomenon and it should not be ignored.

There are many techniques by which this sudden right-brain dominance can be encouraged. Religion has long made use of many of them. Prolonged rhythmic chanting or dancing can produce this effect. That is the point made in the story about the dancing rabbi. Deep meditation can do it; so can fervent prayer. But sometimes it just seems to happen spontaneously. That is what happens when we have a sudden inspiration.

A DIFFERENT KIND
OF KNOWLEDGE

Traditionally many religions have tended to regard the knowledge or insight gained through this sort of flash of inspiration or revelation as a superior form of knowledge, a message from God, and therefore much better than the knowledge arrived at by mere human thought. But we now can see that this sort of knowledge comes as the result of the increased activity of the right brain. It is a form of thought—

thought of a different order, thought that takes place in the right, nonverbal half of the brain, but thought nonetheless.

Religion and rationalism have often clashed over which form of gaining knowledge is best. To advance the case for one form of knowledge at the expense of the other is both unwise and potentially dangerous. Ornstein says that both of these forms of thought must be used. Rational thought cannot resolve all problems, but inspirations are not always correct, and they are usually incomplete.

The California psychologist explains that many of his own ideas come to him by inspiration. But as such they are rarely more than fragmentary images, starting points. It is only when he has brought his intellect—his left-brain activity —to bear on these vague inspirations that they can become useful to others. He concludes: "But a complete human consciousness should include both modes of thought, just as a complete day includes both light and darkness. Perhaps the knowledge that the two modes have a physiological basis will help science and psychology to regain their balance. We must not ignore the right-hemisphere talents of imagination, perspective, and intuition, which in the long run may prove essential to our personal and cultural survival."

FIVE RULES FOR TWO BRAINS

Like most people in the West, you are probably left-brain dominant. You tend to rely on your verbal and logical skills. But, like most people, you are probably influenced by your right-brain activity—perhaps more frequently than you are aware of. It is in your best interest to use both sides of your brain as effectively as possible. Here are some tips for doing so:

1. Don't scorn those "illogical" flashes of inspiration.

Recognize them as a full partner in your brain activity.

2. Don't rationalize inspirations, trying to make them into something they are not. That merely distorts them.

3. Remember that while inspiration may be a good starting point, it is usually incomplete. For an inspiration to grow into a good workable idea a lot of hard logical work may have to follow.

4. Remember also that the inspiration is the product of human brain activity—it is not a divine revelation. Your inspirations can be wrong, just like your logical constructions.

5. While it is only proper to respect other people's inspirations, feelings, tastes, and other illogical conclusions, there is no reason to accept them uncritically. Others have no divine revelation either, and can be just as wrong as you are. There has been no shortage of "inspired madmen" in history.

14

Twenty Final Thoughts

Research has shown that review is the best way to help the brain remember new material. So here is a review, a list of reminders and another of tips. If you remember them and use them properly you will make a good start on getting more out of that marvelous brain of yours. You will begin to think more effectively.

First, here are ten points to remember:

1. Your mind is a pattern-making system. In order to find new solutions you must be able to break the pattern.

2. Don't be afraid to question *every* assumption. *Nothing* is sacred.

3. Everybody, including yourself, has only his own experience to think with.

4. You do *not* see what I see. We all tend to see, hear, and remember what we want to see, hear, and remember. Our view of the world is highly selective.

RE: THINKING

5. If you can't be wrong, you can't be right. Don't be afraid to be wrong sometimes, and don't be afraid to admit it.

6. You will never change anybody's mind on an important issue by arguing with him.

7. Abstractions and generalizations sound good, but they can be very troublesome and misleading. In thinking try to be as concrete and specific as possible.

8. The mind—yours, mine, and everyone else's—tends to defend itself by shutting out what it finds unpleasant or painful. This is a natural process.

9. Don't underestimate your own intuitions, or overestimate the intuitions of others.

10. Intuition is only a starting point. Most bright ideas must be developed and tested—and they often turn out to be wrong.

Now here are ten useful tips that you should commit to memory.

1. Your memory is lousy. When you want to remember something accurately, write it down.

2. Everybody else's memory is lousy too. The past as we remember it is an imaginative reconstruction. When you need accurate information, rely as much as you can on written or printed sources.

3. Know the time of day when your mind works best and try to arrange your schedule accordingly.

4. Don't be afraid to consider a ridiculous idea. Don't reject anything out of hand. Who knows where it might lead?

5. If you feel frustrated by a problem, don't worry. That feeling is natural. Try to think about something else for a while, or sleep on it.

6. If you are frequently caught up in a worry cycle, learn a meditation technique that will give your mind a rest and help to break the cycle.

TWENTY FINAL THOUGHTS

7. With any difficult problem, try to get different points of view. Talk it over with others.

8. Write your problem and options down as clearly and simply as possible.

9. Examine motives, your own as well as other people's. "Why does somebody want me to believe this? Why do I want to believe [or disbelieve] it?"

10. Keep in mind that all words have two definitions, a dictionary definition and an emotional definition—and when trying to make yourself understood, make sure you know both of them.

Books That Can
Help

THE BRAIN

Ferguson, Marilyn. *The Brain Revolution*. New York: Taplinger Publishing Co., 1973.

Jonas, Gerald. *Visceral Learning*. New York: Viking Press, 1973.

Pines, Maya. *The Brain Changers*. New York: Harcourt Brace Jovanovich, 1973.

Russell, Peter. *The Brain Book*. New York: Hawthorn Books, 1979.

PROBLEM SOLVING

Dale, Arbie, and Snow, Leida. *Twenty Minutes a Day to a More Powerful Intelligence*. Chicago: Playboy Press, 1976.

de Bono, Edward. *The Five Day Course in Thinking*. New York: Harper & Row, Publishers, 1973.

——. *Lateral Thinking*. New York: Harper & Row, Publishers, 1970.

Wertheimer, Max. *Productive Thinking*. New York: Harper & Row, Publishers, 1959.

LOGIC AND ARGUMENT

Capaldi, Nicholas. *The Art of Deception*. Buffalo, N.Y.: Prometheus Books, 1979.

Chase, Stuart. *Guides to Straight Thinking*. New York: Harper & Row, Publishers, 1956.

Flesch, Rudolf. *The Art of Clear Thinking*. New York: Harper & Row, Publishers, 1951.

Flew, Antony. *Thinking Straight*. Buffalo, N.Y.: Prometheus Books, 1977.

Ruchlis, Hy. *Clear Thinking*. New York: Harper & Row, Publishers, 1962.

COMMUNICATION

Chase, Stuart. *The Tyranny of Words*. New York: Harcourt Brace Jovanovich, 1938.

Fast, Julius. *Body Language*. New York: M. Evans and Co., 1970.

Whorf, B. L. *Language, Thought and Reality*. New York: John Wiley & Sons, 1956.

INTUITION AND INSIGHT

Buzan, Tony. *Use Both Sides of Your Brain*. New York: E. P. Dutton, 1977.

Ornstein, Robert. *The Mind Field*. New York: Viking Press, 1976.

———. *The Psychology of Consciousness*. New York: Viking Press, 1973.

RATIONALIZING

Aronson, Elliot. *The Social Animal*. 2d ed. San Francisco: W. H. Freeman & Co., 1976.

MEDITATION AND RELAXATION

Benson, Herbert. *The Relaxation Response*. New York: William Morrow & Co., 1975.

Luce, Gay Gaer. *Biological Rhythms in Human and Animal Physiology*. New York: Dover Publications, 1971.

Luce, Gay Gaer, and Segal, Julius. *Sleep*. New York: Coward, McCann & Geoghegan, 1976.

GENERAL

Smith, Adam. *Powers of the Mind*. New York: Random House, 1975.

Viscott, David S. *How to Make Winning Your Lifestyle*. New York: Peter H. Wyden, 1972.

Weinland, James D. *How to Improve Your Memory*. New York: Barnes and Noble Books, 1957.

Index

INDEX

INDEX

INDEX